Praise

THE
THIRD OPTION

"In a time where our country seems more divided racially and politically than at any other in recent history, we need a voice of reason to bring us to a place of understanding. I believe that Miles McPherson is that voice. . . . I can't stress enough how important this work is and hope that it becomes a central part of the conversation going forward. Get the book, devour the concepts, and be part of the change."

—Greg Surratt, founding pastor of
Seacoast Church and president of
the Association of Related Churches (ARC)

"A discussion about race that we desperately need . . . a must read."

—Bishop T. D. Jakes, senior pastor,
the Potter's House

"This is a landmark book, offering a compelling vision for the great issue of our day. Miles helps us to see God's glory and the beauty of his image in everyone we meet. Read this book, then buy copies for all your friends. This message could change everything."

—Rick Warren, author of
The Purpose Driven Life

"The most profound message on reconciliation and healing that I have heard. It is a message that needs to be echoed throughout the world. . . . This is a moment and a movement that you have to be a part of!"

—John Gray, senior pastor of Relentless Church

"Pastor Miles's words will encourage you with a new compassion and new understanding of the heart of God for all people and equip you with the tools to help bring about change."

—Christine Caine, bestselling author and founder of A21 and Propel Women

"Every believer who wants to follow Christ's example to love our neighbors as ourselves must read this book."

—Chris Hodges, senior pastor of Church of the Highlands and author of *Fresh Air* and *The Daniel Dilemma*

"*The Third Option* is exactly what we need to be reminded of. This is how JESUS wants us to live. Rather than separate ourselves by racism, we need to be one race united by love. We are all one people, one human world, all equal."

—Adrián González, former member of the New York Mets

"A powerful and inspirational book. Chock-full of stories, anecdotes, and wisdom that helps readers to build bridges across the great divides of race and ethnicity."

—Dr. David Anderson, senior pastor of Bridgeway Community Church and author of *Gracism: The Art of Inclusion*

"*The Third Option* will not just inspire you; it will equip you with the necessary tools to advance, facilitate, and usher in a spirit of unity. You will not just be blessed, you will be transformed."

—Sam Rodriguez, president of the National Hispanic Church Leadership Conference (NHCLC)

THE
THIRD OPTION

HOPE FOR A RACIALLY DIVIDED NATION

MILES McPHERSON

HOWARD BOOKS

ATRIA

New York   London   Toronto   Sydney   New Delhi

This book is dedicated to my parents, Rudolf and Margaret McPherson, who taught me how to love unconditionally, in spite of the pain that racism inflicted on their lives and the lives of their parents.

Howard Books
An Imprint of Simon & Schuster, Inc.
1230 Avenue of the Americas
New York, NY 10020

First Howard Books paperback edition February 2020

HOWARD BOOKS/ATRIA PAPERBACK and colophon are trademarks of Simon & Schuster, Inc.

For information about special discounts for bulk purchases, please contact Simon & Schuster Special Sales at 1-866-506-1949 or business@simonandschuster.com.

The Simon & Schuster Speakers Bureau can bring authors to your live event. For more information or to book an event, contact the Simon & Schuster Speakers Bureau at 1-866-248-3049 or visit our website at www.simonspeakers.com.

Interior design by Davina Mock-Maniscalco

Manufactured in the United States of America

5   7   9   10   8   6   4

Library of Congress Cataloging-in-Publication Data is available.

ISBN 978-1-5011-7219-9
ISBN 978-1-5011-7220-5 (pbk)
ISBN 978-1-5011-7221-2 (ebook)

Contents

One of the unavoidable characteristics of the NFL is uncertainty. You never know who will be on your team from year to year. Even after the final roster is set, players get hurt, traded, or released, so you often end the season with many different players than you began with. Given that uncertainty, there are two keys to the success I've experienced over the course of my career.

#1: I believe there is an element of greatness inside every person

Believe me when I tell you that I've played with guys from every possible walk of life. Countless cultural and experiential differences exist between us, but there is one thing we all have in common: an invisible source of greatness buried deep inside. This endless well of untapped passion and drive to accomplish more than we ever thought possible, especially in the most difficult of times, is also the stuff that glues us together and makes us closer than brothers. As one of their leaders, my responsibility is to draw out that greatness by speaking life into it, and help my teammates realize there is more in them than they even realize, to do whatever I can to bring out the very best in my teammates.

#2: Trust the process

The better we prepare together, the more we win together.

The normal NFL practice on the field is about two hours long, but the time we spend in meetings preparing is many times that. We watch recorded film to study the tendencies and habits of our opponents and our teammates before and after practice each day. In addition, there are countless hours of "extra" off-the-field mental prep. When I first entered the league, I did much of my extra off-the-field prep alone. But I began to notice that the more extra off-the-field preparation I did with my teammates, the more unified we became. This prep time is as much to learn about ourselves as it is to learn about our opponents. It is arduous and tedious at times, but critical to our success as a team.

Healing the racial divide will not be easy, but what great accomplishment is?

If there is one thing our country needs right now, it is a message that instills a belief in every individual that there is an infinite amount of unseen and untapped greatness in every person we meet. *The Third Option* is that message.

We also need practical steps to follow in our efforts to grow in our understanding of one another. We must move past talking about our differences and begin *living out our similarities*. *The Third Option* is the book that teaches us how to do that. This is not a book for "those people" but for "we the people."

There are countless amazing athletes in the NFL, and I've learned that the ones who win aren't always the most talented. Rather, they're the ones who, along with their teammates, never take their eyes off of their goals, and put in the "extra" hard work and commitment, no matter what they feel in the moment.

Uniting our country will require commitment, sacrifice, and humility, but so does anything great. Anything less is below the value and *standard* of greatness that deep down we all possess.

Don't just read this book, *live this book*.

—Drew Brees

The Third Option

N* or White Boy?

Did they just call me the N-word? School was out, and I rode my bike as fast as I could through the white neighborhood that stood between me and the safety of home.

My heart pounded as I approached an intersection and faced a red light. *Please turn green, please turn green,* I repeated in my head. Just in the nick of time, it did. *Thank you, God!* I crossed the street that served as the gateway into my neighborhood, and zoomed down the hill. I was ten blocks from home.

But I couldn't slow down yet. In fact, entering my Black neighborhood only meant that I'd exited one potential danger zone and entered another.

"Hey, White boy!" someone called. These words shot through my body like adrenaline, making me feel fearful and anxious all over again. I flew through the streets I knew so well, trying to outpace the name-calling, threats, and insults. I didn't slow down until I was two blocks from my house.

I grew up in a predominantly Black neighborhood called Lakeview, in Long Island, New York. But from first through eighth grade, I went to school in an all-White neighborhood called Malverne.

At the time, according to my uncle, the one and only black family who moved to Malverne was welcomed warmly—with a burning cross on their front lawn. So it is easy to understand why I never felt comfortable there.

Ocean Avenue ran between Lakeview and Malverne. Each time I pedaled across Ocean Avenue, I experienced anxiety. On this particular day, I had a legitimate reason to: some White kids from Malverne were chasing me out of their neighborhood. I was pedaling as fast as I could to outrun their threats of violence.

So imagine my devastation when—just as I entered the apparent safe haven of my own neighborhood—I heard the words *Hey, White boy!* As a multiracial kid, I felt like a ping-pong ball bouncing between two worlds, never feeling like I completely belonged to either.

I'm what Black people call a "high yella brother with good hair." To some, that meant I wasn't "black enough." *White boy* was the not-so-affectionate term by which some Black kids in the neighborhood called me. The White kids used even less endearing terms to describe me.

Growing up, I felt like a perpetual outsider. Aside from my parents' home, where diversity was embraced and celebrated, it seemed like there was nowhere I could go to fit in. And though it's been decades since my school days in Lakeview, I still experience the same feelings today from time to time that I did back then.

You may be feeling like I did that day, wondering how you can escape the devastating impacts of racism. Maybe you've experienced racism personally, or know someone else who has. Maybe you feel like you've been wrongly blamed for racist events that happened long before you were born. Maybe you want to learn how to have a conversation about race but you're afraid of saying the wrong thing. Maybe you're trying to recover from the shame of being the target or a perpetrator of racism. Or maybe you're searching for a way to deal with the race-based hate, resentment, and fear you cling to in your heart.

Whatever your reasons for picking up this book, I commend you for your courage and commitment to tackling racism head-on. I have struggled with most of the issues listed above, too, and look forward to sharing what I've learned with you.

Above all, I want to offer you *hope*. Racial unity is God's idea, and He promises that if we ask Him for help, He will be faithful to answer us. Let's approach God with confidence and vulnerability while we trust him to guide us in tackling this issue together.

About Me

My name is Miles McPherson, and I am the senior pastor of the Rock Church, located in "America's Finest City": San Diego, California.

I am the proud offspring of two Black grandfathers, a half-Chinese and half-Black grandmother, and a White grandmother. I am of mixed race, but I identify myself as Black. Consequently, the stories and feelings I share in this book are shared through the lens of a Black man.

I'm also a former NFL player. My love affair with football started when I was a kid. Every Sunday during football season, my dad, uncles, and neighbors played pickup games in the park. Even as a child, when I had the ball in my hands, no one, not even the adults, could catch me. At least, that's how I remember it.

Football came naturally, and I loved every minute that I played, whether in the neighborhood or under stadium lights. In my youth I played in Pop Warner leagues, on my high school team, and at the University of New Haven, where I was the school's first all-American and its first player to be drafted by and to play in the NFL.

Playing football helped me cultivate a strong sense of unity with others from an early age. I've always played with guys who represented all ethnicities and socioeconomic backgrounds. Going to battle with my teammates created a bond between us that bridged our differences.

Football is a great tool for teaching us that what is most powerful and valuable *about* a person is what's on the *inside*, not the *outside*.

Ultimately, it was also football that led me to Jesus. Having attended Catholic school all my life, I learned about God at an early age but walked away from religion after the eighth grade. One night when I was nineteen years old, while I was standing in a department store waiting for my girlfriend to get off work, two hippies who looked like Charles Manson shared the gospel with me. Learning that I was created to have a personal relationship with Jesus rocked my world, and I prayed to receive Christ as my Savior on the spot. For about ten days or so, I was in "spiritual shock." I did not get high on drugs, I stopped having sex, and spent all day wondering what God wanted to do with my life.

The "high" I felt from my newfound relationship with Jesus eventually went away. Since I didn't know anyone who could guide me in the growth of my faith, I returned to my old ways: partying, sleeping around, and living a wild and out-of-control lifestyle. When I joined the San Diego Chargers, I dialed it up even further.

During my first two years in the NFL, I was a "guy gone wild." I smoked a lot of marijuana, used cocaine, and chased women. But all the while, I watched two of my teammates, Sherman Smith and Ray Preston, from afar. Those two Christian men modeled the heart of God and started challenging me to grow in my faith.

On April 12, 1984, at 5:00 a.m., I was lying on a couch in my apartment, my heart pounding in my chest. I'd been using cocaine all night. I was thinking about what those Jesus-loving hippies and my teammates, Sherman and Ray, had said and modeled for me. That morning I recommitted my life to Jesus and never touched cocaine or marijuana again. I reunited with my old girlfriend later that afternoon, and we were married five months later. I played two more years with the Chargers and became known as "the Jesus guy."

When my four-year career with the Chargers ended, I felt the call of God on my heart to serve in ministry. I served as a youth pastor for eight years, and launched Miles Ahead Youth Crusades. Tens of thousands of kids, representing all different racial and socioeconomic backgrounds, came to know Jesus personally through the ministries I led and worked in. I had finally discovered God's true purpose for my life.

Eventually, I took over the Sunday night service at Horizon Christian Fellowship, which grew from six hundred people to over three thousand in five years. Again, these services were as diverse as our city. The Rock Church, which I later founded and of which I am now pastor, is attended, in person and online, by over twenty thousand people weekly. I'm proud of the fact that our congregation is as diverse as a bag of Skittles: 48 percent White, 28 percent Latino, 14 percent Black, 7 percent Asian, and 3 percent other ethnicities. These percentages are neither intentional nor accidental.

When we launched the Rock Church, my staff and I committed ourselves to reaching everybody in the city. We based our commitment on two foundational truths: first, that we are *all* made in the image of God; and second, that the church should reflect the reality that all nations will be gathered in heaven. To this day, we remain committed to these principles, and have extended our reach to five campuses and thirteen microsites, including one in Tijuana and one at a local juvenile detention center and a state prison. Through our online ministry, millions have heard the gospel, and we have recorded over one million decisions for Christ.

A lifetime of experiences—growing up a mixed-race kid in a segregated era of our nation's history, living in diverse neighborhoods and cities, playing on a diverse NFL team, and pastoring multiethnic congregations—has given me a deeper understanding of God's heart for his people to live in loving unity. My highest calling is to love others the way Jesus calls us to. While I've failed in that endeavor more times than I can count, my greatest desire is to grow more perfect in love, especially toward those who don't look like me. This book is my earnest attempt to help you do the same.

The stories and perspectives I share are meant to answer the many questions I've been posed as a Black pastor of a large, urban, multiracial church. Well-meaning people of all backgrounds want to understand the racial issues that divide our nation, and what they can do to alleviate them. This book is my effort at answering their questions and encouraging us to honor each other and ourselves the way God does.

The Third Option: Honor

Do you find yourself getting angry or defensive when you think or talk about race? Do you look at the racial divide and wish there was a solution? Do you, like Rodney King, ask why we all can't get along? If so, I want you to know that (1) you are not alone, (2) racism corrupts our souls, (3) culture promotes racism, and (4) there's a Third Option that can set us free.

Everyone is affected by racism. Nearly every American has been a victim or a perpetrator of racism, and most have been both. On average, 83 percent of Americans believe racism is a problem in our nation. This number has remained steady over the past two decades, with the latest polls showing a spike in the percentage of Americans—now 58 percent—who believe that racism is a "big problem."[1]

You may despise racism, but it affects us all, whether we know it or not. It is a corruptor of the soul that degrades and devalues those who look different from us. When we allow racism into our hearts and society, we minimize the priceless value of God's image in others, which limits our ability to honor, love, and serve them the way God calls us to.

Culture plays a big role in perpetuating racism by wrongly insisting that there are only two options you can choose from: us or them.

Culture pits one group of people against another by promoting a zero-sum-game mentality that says, "You must lose in order for me to win."

God, however, offers us a Third Option that stands in stark contrast to the two offered by culture. God's Third Option invites us to honor that which we have in common, the presence of His image in every person we meet. When we honor the presence of His image in others, we acknowledge their priceless value as precious and beloved of God. The Third Option empowers us to see people through God's eyes, which enables us to treat them in a manner that honors the potential of His image in us.

Some of the greatest heroes of our faith overcame culture's temptation to buy into the us-versus-them mentality. One example in the Old Testament is Joshua. As Joshua prepared for the battle of Jericho, he asked an approaching messenger of the Lord to identify whose "side" he was on:

> Now when Joshua was near Jericho, he looked up and saw a man standing in front of him with a drawn sword in his hand. Joshua went up to him and asked, "Are you for us or for our enemies?"
>
> "Neither," he replied, "but as commander of the army of the Lord I have now come." Then Joshua fell facedown to the ground in reverence, and asked him, "What message does my Lord have for his servant?" (Joshua 5:13-14)

In this passage, the Lord's messenger offered Joshua a way out of culture's trap by giving him a Third Option. Joshua responded to the presence of God in humility and obedience, and reaped the benefits of God's blessings in return. God personally intervened on Joshua's behalf to deliver him an overwhelming victory at Jericho, because Joshua decided to choose the Third Option.

Choosing the Third Option in our hearts and culture isn't easy; it requires intentionality, a prayerful commitment to obedience, and wholehearted trust in God's provision. But I promise you it's worth the effort. When we choose the Third Option, God Himself will deliver us from an us-versus-them mentality that prevents us from honoring the presence of His image in ourselves and in others.

Works in Progress

The Third Option is more than a choice; it's a God-given mission that directs us to honor our neighbors the way that God calls us to.

Culture, on the other hand, asks us to determine whether the issue of race is something we should even concern ourselves with in the first place. Culture does this by posing an oversimplified question—Are you a racist?—and forcing us to choose yes or no in response. A small percentage of Americans would answer yes. Most of us would say no, because we're either unaware of or unwilling to admit our biases, biases that we all have, even if they are subconscious.

Consequently, we're likely to answer "no" in one of the following ways:

Defensiveness: I'm not a racist. I may have some biases, but they're all justified, and that doesn't amount to racism.

Self-righteousness: I'm not a racist. I'm a social crusader who's "woke." ("Woke" is slang for being aware of issues pertaining to racial and social justice.)

Helplessness: I'm not a racist, and there's nothing I can do about racism in America.

Apathy: I'm not a racist, and racism doesn't concern me.

Uncertainty: I'm not a racist, and I'm not entirely sure what "being racist" means.

The Third Option frees us from culture's false dichotomy by offering us the grace we need in order to admit that we are imperfect in our love for others. The Third Option opens the eyes of our hearts so that we can acknowledge biases where they exist. And the Third Option enables us to define who we want to become, so that we can wholeheartedly pursue our God-given mission to love and honor all our neighbors equally. The Third Option acknowledges that my biases will do and say racist things, but I can learn to live more honorably.

Me, You, We

I've seen firsthand how racism affects individuals and communities and impacts us in different ways. I've witnessed racism erode our ability to live in unity with others and prevent us from recognizing the loving image of God in ourselves. I believe racism can only be conquered when individuals take ownership and responsibility for their own attitudes, words, and actions; when another's experience is understood and honored; and when we decide to tackle racism together. To illustrate this, I have set up the book in three parts: Me, You, and We.

Me: If I want to be an agent for change, I must first purify my own heart. Or, as Scripture more bluntly says, I must first remove the plank from my own eye before I can see clearly enough to remove the speck from my brother's. In this section, we'll ask God to reveal racial blind spots that prevent us from honoring others, what role we play in perpetuating racism, and what God is calling us to do about it.

You: With the plank removed from my own eye, I can now see you more clearly. But in order to really understand your experience, I must step out of my comfort zone and into your shoes. Walking in another's shoes is never a comfortable experience, but it's essential to understanding their perspective and learning how to honor them. In this section, we'll explore what it feels like to be the "other" and learn to empathize with those who've been marginalized by racism.

We: Our lives, joys, and burdens are meant to be shared in community. As Scripture says, "Two are better than one, because they have a good return for their labor. If either of them falls down, one can help the other up . . . Though one may be overpowered, two can defend themselves. A cord of three strands is not easily broken" (Ecclesiastes 4:9–12). In this section, we'll identify ways that we can edify and honor each other as a church, a city, a community, and a country.

This book will challenge and encourage you to choose the Third Option so that you can achieve an elevated level of honor that is consistent with the priceless value of God's image in you and your brothers and sisters of all races and ethnicities. But in order for real transformation to occur, you must be open to a new level of vulnerability with the Holy Spirit. Unity is God's idea and can only be achieved by the Holy Spirit's transformation of our hearts. I ask you to join me in prayer as we seek to honor God's heart for unity.

Prayer

Lord, please prepare my heart for what I am about to read. Holy Spirit, just as a seed cannot grow into a plant unless it is planted and dies, please reveal what needs to die in me, so that You may grow a desire in my heart to move past my comfort zone and love others like You love them. Holy Spirit, I give you permission to expose that which needs to be transformed in me, and I ask You to change my heart, attitude, and actions for your glory and benefit.

In the name of our Lord, Amen.

PART I

FRAMING THE PROBLEM

At the beginning of every sermon I deliver, I try to make sure my audience and I are on the same page regarding what it is, exactly, that we're talking about. This is especially important when we're discussing an emotional issue like racism. Racism affects everyone differently, making it difficult to be objective about what actions, words, and thoughts are considered "racist."

In the next two chapters, I'll lay the foundation for my operating definition of racism by explaining what racism looks, sounds, and feels like, and why racism runs counter to God's commandment to love and honor the presence of His image in everyone we meet.

CHAPTER 1

Fifty Shades of Brown

"Yo, man, what are *you?"*

I remember lining up in a stairwell at school with a bunch of my White classmates. I was about ten years old. Someone called me the N-word, and I froze. *Oh, man, what do I do? I'm surrounded by all these White kids!* But we all got along, so I didn't *do* anything, and I don't remember what I said. I just remember feeling frozen and scared.

Sadly, it wasn't unusual for me to hear this word. At my school, there were only two or three Blacks in my class, and the other kids constantly made racial comments about us.

On another occasion, around the same time, I was at a classmate's house, playing in his backyard. His mom was there, and he looked at her and said, "Watch this." Suddenly he turned to me and called me the N-word, out of the blue. Again, it had a paralyzing effect on me, almost like a curse.

You feel guilty when you *do* something wrong, but you feel shame when you feel like you *are* something wrong. In that moment I felt shame. I felt inferior. I felt weak. I felt powerless. And his mom did nothing, which only affirmed his judgment of me as a N*.

I felt powerless against the N-word, which hovered over my head like a cloud. And that cloud wasn't limited to my head; it permeated the whole culture. It was on TV, in the media, and in sports. You saw Muhammad Ali and Martin Luther King Jr. dealing with it. It was a constant reminder that "we" were different from "them."

But while White kids called me the N-word, Blacks questioned the authenticity of my Blackness. Since I was a mixed-race kid, they wondered if I was *really* Black and questioned whether I was capable of sharing their racial experience.

My best friend growing up was a Black kid named Mike. One day, when we were teenagers, I was standing in front of his house with his dad, and his dad told me, "You are going to have it easier than Mikey because *the White man gonna love you.*" He thought that because white people could see part of themselves in me, they would consider me "safer" than those who were dark, like his son. In essence, he was telling me that I wouldn't experience the full weight of Mike's disadvantage because of my lighter skin.

When African Americans say that I'm not really Black, it can come across as a matter-of-fact statement, as a joke, or as resentment, but the general sentiment is *You have it easier, because you're mixed.* And that's true sometimes.

When White people say, *You're not really Black,* they're saying that in their mind they have a picture of what Black is, and I don't quite fit that image. However, I'm only a quarter White, so while I may have it easier than some dark-skinned people, I don't have the full identity of a White person either.

The message I got from both sides was the same: *You're not really one of us because we don't share the same exact skin tone.* But is skin tone really a legitimate basis for determining our similarities and differences?

The Science of Unity

I'd answer the question with an unequivocal *NO*, based on the science underlying our genetic makeup. Did you know that all of humankind shares a genome that is 99.5 percent identical?[2]

Biologically speaking, we're all the same. There is as little genetic diversity within a race as there is between races. This means that race is a social construct. There is only one race—the human race.

By design, we have more in common and are more connected than we are different and divided. When we believe this, we can start truly developing a culture of unity that aligns with our genetic reality.

What Can Brown Do for You?

Melanin is a brown substance that gives our skin and hair its color. It also gives color to the irises of our eyes. Those with darker skin have higher amounts of melanin.

The reason "Black don't crack" (an urban saying describing the fact that people with a high degree of melanin have fewer wrinkles) is because melanin protects the skin from the sun's damaging ultraviolet rays. The more pigment you have, the more sun your skin can withstand.

Since the shade of our skin, or melanin content, is also determined by our exposure to the sun, our appearance adjusts to the climate in minor ways. God covered us with one skin color and gave us the ability to be temporarily transformed into a deeper, darker one in the summer. It's called a "tan."

Countless people go to Hawaii to get the perfect tan, only to come home and show it off. No one gets a tan intending to hide it! So how weird would it be if you walked into a room, still blissfully "aloha"-ed out, ten shades of brown darker than when you left, and nobody said a word? Wouldn't you be upset if everyone ignored your perfect tan?

Yet, when someone is *born* with a "tan," that's exactly what people pretend to do. They act like they don't notice it, and get uncomfortable talking about or referencing it. Their reactions made me realize that it's not the *shade* of brown that people don't see; it's *origin* of it that people don't want to address.

God made melanin so that His creative genius could be seen in various shades of brown. Even what we call White and Black are simply very light and very dark shades of brown. For this reason, I believe that we are all just different shades of the same color.

Another Shade of Brown

I have always had a heart for prisoners, and have visited prisons and juvenile detention centers all around the world since 1984. Every time I visit, I'm always struck by just how segregated prisons are. For the most part, Whites hang together with Whites, Blacks with Blacks, Asians with Asians, Pacific Islanders with Pacific Islanders, and Latinos with Latinos. You see a few interracial friendships here and there, but there are strong expressions, and expectations, of racial division overall.

On this particular day, three White dudes were walking around a track that circled the yard. As they approached, I could see they were White supremacists. One guy was ahead of the other two, who were on his right and left. Racist tattoos covered their bodies. They walked around the track declaring to everyone: *This is who we are. Deal with it.*

I said to myself, *I'm going to talk to those guys.* As they came by, I walked over to the track and called them over. Not only did they come over to me, the leader got within three inches of my face. I said to him, "Hey, man, Jesus wants you."

"What are you talking about?" he growled back.

"Jesus wants you. He wants your life."

We stood nose to nose for about sixty seconds.

I initiated this exchange for two reasons. First, because God loves him, and Jesus really did want his heart. Second, I knew that genetically, we were 99.5 percent identical, and therefore we were more similar than we were different.

That guy had the ability to know God and experience His love and forgiveness in the same way that I do. He may have had a lot more obstacles because of his culture and his experiences, but he still had the potential to know and receive God's love.

Instead, he walked away. He and his posse resumed their march, projecting their *White is right, Black get back, Brown stay down* strut.

As he walked away, I wondered what this White supremacist would think if he realized he was just a lighter shade of my skin tone. I wondered if anything would change if he knew we shared the same genes and that, when we stood nose to nose, he and I were practically looking in a genetic mirror.

Mistaken Identity

We are all of mixed race, to some degree. Given that we live in a nation of immigrants, you would rarely find any American who is 100 percent "ethnically pure."

In the twentieth century, a classification of race was developed called the "one-drop rule." Based on a desire to maintain a pure White race, those in power determined that if someone had just "one drop of black blood," they were Black. This classification was reinforced with Jim Crow laws in the Reconstruction Era following the Civil War.[3]

Recently, I was flipping through channels and paused on an episode of the *George Lopez* show. Lopez was curious about the true ethnic makeup of several celebrities. He had them submit a saliva sample to a lab, which traced their ancestry. When he unveiled their results on the show, everyone was surprised.

According to the test results, Jessica Alba, a caramel-skinned beauty who could pass as almost any ethnicity, is 13 percent Native American and 87 percent European.

George Lopez, who's best known as a Latino comedian, is 55 percent European, 32 percent Native American, 9 percent East Asian, and 4 percent sub-Saharan African.

The iconic rapper Snoop Dogg, a brown-skinned African American who shaped an entire generation of hip hop, is 71 percent sub-Saharan African, 23 percent Native American, and 6 percent European.

Celebrities aren't the only ones who are shocked by their DNA results. A few years ago, a White Supremacist leader named Craig Cobb agreed to take a DNA test. When the results of his test were revealed on a nationally syndicated talk show, they indicated that he was 14 percent sub-Saharan African. In other words, the brother was part black![4]

As these real life stories show, most people don't know their genetic makeup and end up fighting against people who are actually just like them. It's sad that we spend so much energy defending our unknown and often mistaken identities.

If you discovered that a measurable portion of your genetic makeup was of a race *different* from the one you identify with, would that change how you viewed others? Would you come to realize that you've been biased against yourself?

The reality is, almost all of us would be surprised to know the truth about our ancestry, since we learn from an early age to identify ourselves and others as Black, White, or another shade of Brown. More important, when God beholds us, all He sees is that we're made in His image, and equally loved.

My genetic makeup turns out to be 50.2 percent sub-Saharan African, 31.8 percent European, 16.7 percent East Asian, 0.7 percent Middle Eastern and North African, and 0.5 percent unassigned. I identify as Black, but I know that God sees me—and everyone else in this world—as simply "beloved."

Let me challenge you to start each day by looking in the mirror and admiring your skin color. Whether it's dark, light, or somewhere in between, acknowledge and praise God for the beauty of his artistic design on your skin.

The Color White

In an episode of the 1970s Black comedy called *Sanford and Son*, Fred G. Sanford, played by the actor Redd Foxx, was robbed. During the police interview, Fred is asked, "Was the perpetrator colored?" to which Fred replies, "Yeah, he was colored white!"

This comedic clip reaffirms our assessment of White being a color of its own. White is a cultural identity that's as distinct as Black, Latino, Asian, or Pacific Islander. But in our conversations on race, we often refer to White people as one group versus "everyone else."

Throughout this book, I make distinctions between White people and people of color, because it's the primary racial paradigm that we live and operate within. When my White friends are left out of discussions focused on "people of color," they often wonder where they'll fit in as the country becomes more and more diverse. The word *inclusion*, to them, often feels like exclusion. They wonder if they'll have a seat at the table as we tackle the issue of racism together. The answer must be *yes*, for we must recognize White as a color, associated with its own blessings and burdens, just like every other color.

Everyone Sees Color, Even Jesus

Even though we're more alike than we are different, it would be naïve to pretend that ethnicity is not a real thing. Humans are all different, and it would be disingenuous—even dishonest—to pretend otherwise. I learned this in a very memorable way many years ago. It was 1982, a few days after I was drafted to the NFL's Los Angeles Rams. I boarded a flight in New Haven, Connecticut, on my way to California. Changing planes in Las Vegas, I noticed a guy in the airport who I initially thought was a *really* big, light-skinned Black dude.

As I got closer, I realized he was in an extreme category of big! And he wasn't exactly a Black brother—he was something else. He had my complexion, was about an inch taller than me, was twice as wide and a hundred pounds heavier. But I was clueless as to his ethnicity.

Maybe he's just a huge Puerto Rican? Nah. I had to know, so I walked up and introduced myself. And with a low, silky-smooth voice, he answered, "I'm Junior."

Now I was really confused. He had no Spanish accent and didn't *sound* like any brothers I knew. I'd never seen a man like this in my life. Turned out, he was heading to the Los Angeles Rams camp, too.

As we walked onto the plane, he had to turn sideways just to fit down the aisle. When he was halfway to his seat, a tiny elderly woman who reminded me of Betty White turned and saw Junior; her eyes popped in surprise, and she blurted out, "Oh, my!"

That's what I was thinking when I first saw him, too. I eventually said, "Yo, man, what are you?" And with his deep silky voice, he replied, "I'm Samoan, man!"

It would be impossible, irresponsible, and fundamentally dishonest to meet Junior and say, *I don't see his Samoan-ness.*

When someone says, "I don't see color," they are simply ignoring reality. The first time someone said that to me, I was confused. I thought they were literally color-blind. They couldn't actually be saying they didn't see my caramel, Hawaii-tan, Latino wannabe shade of brown skin. No way!

Then I realized they were serious. So I wondered, *What do they see?* It was somewhat insulting that they weren't willing to acknowledge my ethnicity. Certainly they knew their own skin color; were they saying I was White like them?

I get that *I'm color-blind* is an attempt to say *I want to treat everyone the same.* I understand it, and I honor that intention. But claiming not to see color is often viewed by people of color as an attempt to ignore the racial tension that actually exists. It sounds a lot like someone saying *I don't have any issues, so I assume you don't either—and if we don't bring it up, it doesn't exist.* Claiming to be color-blind shuts down attempts at engaging in a meaningful conversation about race. It sends the message that a tan received in Hawaii is celebrated, but a tan received in the womb is invalidated.

We know from the Scriptures that Jesus definitely saw color. While walking to Galilee, Jesus entered a region called Samaria. He went to the well and was met by a local woman. He asked her to give Him a drink, and she acknowledged the racial implications of what he'd asked for by saying, "How is it that You, being a Jew, ask a drink from me, a Samaritan woman?" The verse goes on to say, "For Jews have no dealings with Samaritans."

To contextualize this exchange, hatred between the Jews and Samaritans was pervasive, fierce, and long-standing. Feuds between the two ethnic groups can be traced all the way back to the days of the patriarchs of the Christian faith. Their mutual hatred erupted when, around 530 BC, forty-three thousand members of the nation of Israel—who had previously been carried off into Babylonian captivity—were permitted to return and rebuild Jerusalem in the land occupied by Samaritans. The Samaritans, understandably, opposed the repatriation of their land against their will. Jews, in turn, detested the culture and religion of the Samaritans, calling them "dogs" and "half-breeds."

Given this context, if Jesus had ignored the Samaritan woman's ethnicity by claiming to be color-blind, the significance of his gesture would have been lost. He would have essentially ignored the racial oppression that the Samaritans had experienced at the hands of the Jewish people, and He would have missed an opportunity to illustrate God's love for everyone.

The lesson I gleaned from this story is that we honor God when we honor someone else's inherent, priceless value, including his or her ethnicity. We live up to the standard that God has placed on us as humans when we love people for who they are, even at the expense of potential criticism from those who are "like us," rather than pretend to overlook our differences.

Different Shades of the Same

On the one hand, we've created a problem by claiming we're more different than we actually are. On the other hand, we've created a problem by ignoring our differences.

If we're going to overcome the racial divide in our culture, we must first understand both the nature of our division *and* the potential for unity. We must acknowledge that different shades have different experiences, while recognizing that we all share the same desire to be honored for who we are.

Once we learn who and what we really are, we'll learn how we were designed to treat each other. When we realize we're all basically a creative version of the same design, that knowledge will unite us.

Restoring Broken Pieces

Kintsugi is a Japanese custom of fixing broken pottery as a form of artwork. *Kintsugi* artists believe that when broken pieces of pottery are glued back together, often with pure gold, the result can be even more beautiful and valuable than the original.

Like broken pottery, our racial culture is similarly fractured, and needs repairing. And like those who practice *kintsugi*, God pieces together our broken and humbled hearts with the "gold" of honor. In our culture, honor is the glue that binds and keeps us together. And His resulting masterpiece is indeed stunning.

I know, because I've seen it.

Restoration

We were designed to live in a reality of mutual honoring and loving unity. Allowing racism, discrimination, and fear to drive a wedge between us is not consistent with God's design for our lives. Separation based on physical appearance is living beneath our God-given potential.

The goal is healing—a beautiful restoration of the unity that is broken along racial lines.

God's artistry can be seen in the combination of each person's color, shape, facial features, and even swag. But it's also found in their inner being—their perspectives, their personalities, and their hopes, dreams, and visions for their lives.

Throughout our journey, I will reiterate the importance of acknowledging the outward appearance of an individual as a partial means of understanding who they are on the inside. Together, we'll learn to honor the uniqueness of others and celebrate the beauty of God's artistry in ourselves and in others.

Next Steps

1. Look in the mirror and say, "God made me this way and He made me beautiful." Now say that out loud about a friend who looks different.

2. Take a DNA test—23andMe, MyHeritage, Ancestry, or any other of a number of options you can find through a quick Google search—and discover your true racial makeup.

3. Say the prayer below out loud. There will be one at the end of every chapter.

Prayer

"Lord, I will praise You, for I am fearfully and wonderfully made; Marvelous are Your works . . ." (Psalm 139:14)

Thank you for creating us out of the same genetic material, to remind us that we're all the same. And thanks, also, for expressing your creativity through us in such beautiful and unique ways. Help us see and appreciate ourselves and others for who we really are: your precious children, created in Your image, priceless in value and worthy of honor.

In your powerful name, I pray, Amen.

CHAPTER 2

What Is Racism?

Racism 101

The Anti-Defamation League (ADL) defines *racism* as "the belief that a particular ethnicity is superior or inferior to another, and that a person's social and moral traits are predetermined by his or her inborn biological characteristics."[5]

I'd bet most people in America wouldn't categorize themselves as "racist" based on this definition. After all, we are generally unaware of how ingrained they are in our upbringing and psyches.

But what if *racism* were defined differently? What if *racism* were defined not so much by what you did, felt, or believed about someone of a different race, but by what you *didn't* do, feel, or believe about them?

The Bible says that God created us to honor the priceless value of His image in ourselves and in each other. When we allow our mistaken beliefs about other ethnicities to prevent us from loving them, a different form of racism causes us to *withhold His love* from those God created us *to* love. In other words, racism can be as much of a sin of *omission*—not doing what we are called to do—as a sin of *commission*.

Moreover, racism is equally dishonoring to both its target and its perpetrator, because it dishonors the image of God in all of us. And racism is what naturally occurs when God is pushed out of a relationship. Racism is about one group exercising its power over another based on race and manifested in oppression. Racism is a sin of the heart, and Romans 3:23 says that all have sinned. *All* means *all*: Whites, Blacks, Latinos, Asians, Middle Easterners, and everyone in between. Racism is an equal opportunity offender, a human condition that affects all people.

Racism expresses itself in three ways: institutionally, personally, and internally.[6]

Institutionalized racism

Institutionalized racism exists when one group withholds from another group access to basic needs, such as adequate education, health care, good jobs, political representation, healthy food, and clean water.

The basic necessities of life are withheld based on a perceived need or right to dishonor another people group as a whole. Institutionalized racism is responsible for creating environments that make it more difficult for certain racial groups to take advantage of opportunities afforded to those in power.

Every racial group in America has suffered from this kind of racism.

At the turn of the twentieth century, the Chinese Exclusion Act was passed by Congress and signed into law, and was the first significant law restricting immigration into the United States. These laws remained in effect from 1882 till 1943, and negatively affected the upward social mobility of an entire generation of Chinese Americans in our country. The Chinese were depicted as "parasitic locusts" and the satirical name for a Chinese man was "Ching Chong Ding Dong."[7]

The Irish were targets of racism in early America. In 1798, Congress passed three "Alien Acts" based on fears of Irish Catholics immigrating to the US. Those already living in America were excluded from all parts of civilized society, with signs reading "No Irish Need Apply" hanging in storefronts, and depictions of the Irish as Celtic ape-men with sloping foreheads and monstrous appearances portrayed throughout the media. Historians designated the Irish as "fated to remain a massive lump in the community, undigested, undigestible."[8]

From 1848 to 1928, at least 232 people of Mexican descent were killed by mob lynchings in Texas alone. Latinos were subjected to "Juan Crow" laws that segregated Hispanics and Latinos from White people—with signs reading "We serve Whites only, no Spanish or Mexicans" regularly posted in public establishments. [9]

From 1934 to 1968, the Federal Housing Administration institutionalized racism against Black people through a policy called "redlining."[10] Redlining is the practice of denying or limiting financial services to certain neighborhoods based on their racial or ethnic compositions, without regard for the individual residents' qualifications or creditworthiness. The term *redlining* refers to the practice of using a red line on a map to delineate areas where financial institutions would not invest. The vast majority of redlined neighborhoods were Black neighborhoods, and there is plenty of evidence that the practice still continues today, though in a less overt but equally pernicious manner.

Personally Mediated Racism

Personally mediated racism occurs when one individual dishonors another based on their race. Calling someone a racially derogatory name or denying them an opportunity because of their race are examples of personally mediated racism.

My sister, while working as an interior designer in a private residence, was engaged in small talk with the client as she was packing up her things to leave the client's home. All of a sudden the lady said, "You are a good Negress." I didn't even know that was a word. My sister responded by asking, "What did you say?!" The lady spent sixty seconds mumbling something that was nothing close to an apology. This example of personally mediated racism hit close to home, literally (this happened in modern-day San Diego!) and figuratively.

Internalized Racism

Internalized racism occurs when a person adopts the negative views and labels others have given them. It's also the hardest type of racism to overcome, because it impairs an individual's ability to recognize God's image in themselves.

At the age of thirteen, Jerry came to the United States from Michoacán, Mexico. He secured a job working in the fields, but his accent was so heavy that the Mexican workers who had been in the US longer and considered themselves "Americanized" mocked him, calling him a "Dirty Mexican." The attacks were so bad that he vowed never to subject his family to that form of hatred again. Consequently, he forbade his children from learning Spanish, and then took it further by refraining from eating Mexican food in public.

Today his thirty-one-year-old grandson Travis, who is half-Mexican and half-White, cannot speak Spanish. And because of it, he has been mocked by other Mexican Americans who accuse him of not being Mexican enough. To Whites, he's Mexican; and to Mexicans, he's White (and all I can say is: I *feel* you, brother!). Not only does he not know the language, but he is also disconnected from his Mexican culture.

To this day, Travis has resisted learning Spanish, to avoid being shamed by his own people. Yet he serves as a pastor of one of our most "Latino" campuses, which meets one mile from the Mexican border. Knowing the language would not only help him meet the needs of our congregation, but also help him redeem his God-given identity.

I challenged him to confront the ugly fruit of this internalized racism by learning his grandfather's native language. And I'm proud to report that he recently announced to his congregation his intention of learning Spanish—in spite of deeply ingrained fears that some will criticize him for doing so. Fortunately, he has faith that there will be more who are "for" him than "against" him. This is usually true. The negative voices are usually the loudest and weakest.

Of the three forms of racism, internalized racism is the most devastating, because it messes with our self-worth and hinders our ability to honor others who share our racial identity. To better understand our division, I want to propose a concept that plays a huge role in all three types of racism: groups.

In- and Out-Groups

Courtney grew up in predominantly Black housing projects in Malden, Massachusetts, north of Boston. She attended predominantly Black elementary and junior high schools in her neighborhood. But life drastically changed for her when she and her friends started attending an integrated high school.

She and her Black friends were not readily accepted by the Asian and White students in the school. Like most high school students, she spent her high school years hanging with her group to avoid being shunned by other groups based on race. Courtney had an "in-group" and an "out-group."

In the context of racism, *in-group* and *out-group* are the terms that social scientists use to talk about the us-versus-them dynamic. Culture causes us to sort people into groups that are either "like me" or "not like me."

For those of us who have a healthy sense of self, we subconsciously assume that the "like me" group is better than the "not like me" group.[11]

An in-group can be any group you identify with based on your race, your religion, your gender, or your profession. How you define yourself is how you'll draw the boundaries of your "in-group."

There are also nuances within in-groups. Most groups have their own slang words to describe different kinds of people within their group—terms that their out-groups are not necessarily privy to.

Being light-skinned Black, I was called "yella brother," "high-yella brother," and "redbone" by other Black people.

My Italian friends had nicknames for people who expressed different levels of Italian-ness depending on their hairstyles, clothes, and even their walk. (*Italian-ness* wasn't a word yesterday, but it is now.)

Once we identify our in-group, we tend to apply an "in-group bias." This is the often subconscious tendency for us to give preference to people we perceive as being part of our group. This preferential treatment is associated with an increased level of trust, patience, benefit of the doubt, interest, and comfort around those in our in-group.

Those who aren't part of your in-group are part of your out-group. Those are the people we identify as being "not like me." We tend to be much less familiar, less trusting, less patient, and less interested in members of our out-group.

My eight years in Catholic school were really lonely. I never really felt like I belonged to any particular group. Being one of four Blacks in my class, I never felt completely *in* with most of my schoolmates. The White kids had their parties and their relationships. Their music was different. They watched *American Bandstand* and made fun of *Soul Train*. Very few White kids were into Motown, and I couldn't get into the Eagles. To me, if you weren't down with Stevie Wonder, Smokey Robinson, and the Jackson 5, there was something wrong with your brain.

I remember feeling like our White teachers favored White students as well. They were picked first, they seemed to receive extra attention when asking for help, and they were given a lot more grace when they made mistakes. Most important, when a White kid clearly broke a rule, it seemed to be "okay" or ignored, whereas Black kids would feel the full brunt of a teacher's discipline. In other words, the "in-group" of White students received preference from White teachers, and the "out-group"—everyone else, including me—noticed.

Because of my eight years in Catholic school, I got to know White kids better than the Black kids in my neighborhood knew them. And I noticed that each group made very general and ill-informed comments about the other.

When you don't belong to a certain group, you're relatively limited in your knowledge of them. You may have had one or two personal experiences, but most likely you've been influenced by other people's comments and the media.

In- and Out-Group Bias

When Courtney left Massachusetts and moved to San Diego, the African American group was her in-group, and that's who she gravitated toward. Mexicans were her out-group.

She'd heard many stories about violence by the drug cartels in Mexico and feared the Mexicans in San Diego would bring harm to her. Because they were an out-group, and she had limited exposure to individuals in the group, she generalized her opinions of them based on what she heard in the media or from her in-group.

We all have a tendency to perceive members of an out-group as generally similar to another, and members of our in-group as more unique. This tendency causes us to stereotype and overgeneralize the behaviors and mannerisms of our out-group.

In other words, when we're in a group, we can easily see and understand how the group is diverse. We can see that each person in the group is unique. But when we look at our out-groups, we can only see them from the outside, and we subconsciously tend to believe all the people in those groups are the same.

My White classmates at Catholic school had a general idea of the

Black kids in my neighborhood, but those views were biased. They'd never been to my neighborhood, had never met my African-American friends, and had only anecdotal information about who I was. Because I was in their out-group, they didn't see me; they saw a stereotype of me.

If Latinos are your out-group, you might think all Latinos speak the same language and dialect, eat the same foods, and see the world the same way. You might not realize the difference in accents, words, and phrases that vary from one Latin culture to another.

You might not be able to tell a Korean from a Japanese woman, leading you to offend their social norms or say *thank you* in the wrong language. Or you might take either of them to a Chinese restaurant, thinking you're doing something culturally sensitive.

You might lump all Muslims into one or two categories when there are over 150 different sects of Islam. And you might not even realize that all Arabs aren't Muslim, and not all Muslims are Arab.

The tendency to view, and treat, a person or group of people as intrinsically different from ourselves is referred to as "othering." This shapes our identification and treatment of "those" people. All of this is a dangerous slide into racism, because it overgeneralizes without seeking to understand the nuances that make us so special in God's eyes.

Just as we often subconsciously give preferential treatment to members of our in-group, we tend to withhold it from our out-group. Generally speaking, we are less patient, are less trusting, and avoid building relationships with those in our out-groups.

We also don't give our out-groups the opportunity to show us who they really are, because we've already made up our minds about them. We offer less grace for their mistakes, and we internalize assumptions about who they are, based on almost no personal experience or information.

We also learn quickly from members of our in-group that spending too much time with members of the out-group could threaten our membership in our group.

Out-group and in-group categorization lies at the heart of racism, but thankfully this dynamic also offers a solution: choosing to apply our in-group bias to those in our out-groups.

As you read the list below, imagine your racial in-group—those who are "like you"—and ask yourself if this resonates with how you view and treat them.

1. I am more comfortable with **those like me**.

2. I am more inclined to spend time socially with **those like me**.

3. I am more patient with **those like me**.

4. I give the benefit of the doubt quicker to **those like me**.

5. I express more grace when mistakes are made by **those like me**.

6. It is easier to communicate with **those like me**.

7. I assume I will get along easier with **those like me**.

8. I am more willing to go out of my way to help **those like me**.

9. I possess more positive assumptions about **those like me**.

Does this sound like how you might treat someone you consider to be "like you"?

Now consider how you might treat those in your out-group—those who aren't "like you."

1. I am less comfortable with **those not like me**.

2. I am less inclined to spend time socially with **those not like me**.

3. I am less patient with **those not like me**.

4. I don't give the benefit of the doubt to **those not like me**.

5. I offer less grace to others when mistakes are made by **those not like me**.

6. It is more difficult to communicate with **those not like me**.

7. I don't assume I will get along with **those not like me**.

8. I am less willing to go out of my way to help **those not like me**.

9. I possess fewer positive assumptions about **those not like me**.

The Third Option in Action

Now that you see this comparison, can you see how easily out-group discrimination can be viewed as racism when applied to someone who is part of your racial out-group? What kind of response would you expect if you treated someone like that? How do you think they would feel if they noticed you treating someone else with in-group bias and then experienced out-group discrimination from you?

The good news is that you can take a huge step toward honoring "the other" by intentionally applying in-group bias to those in your out-group. The next time you encounter someone from your racial out-group, take a moment to assess how much out-group discrimination you are inclined to express. Then purposefully apply your in-group bias toward them and see how it changes your ability to honor them, and vice versa.

Learning to "convert" behaviors, words, and attitudes that others experience as racist is critical to learning how to love and honor them.

Sidenote: If at any time while reading this book you feel like you're being labeled a racist—either by me or by yourself—please pause, take a breath, and reflect on the underlying premise of this book. Every person in the world—you, me, and everyone we meet—are flawed human beings with subconsciously biased tendencies toward those in our out-group. Bias is just one of many manifestations of our fallen, imperfect natures.

The Third Option is meant to free you from owning the "racist" label, by encouraging you to recognize and acknowledge that we are all works in progress. The Third Option unequivocally affirms you are not defined by your "transitory" behaviors, thoughts, or attitudes, and that God is actively helping you become the loving, honoring person you were created to be.

We're All One Group

We can only nurture unity by honoring the value that God places on each of us. *Honor assigns value* to someone, regardless of who they are, what they look like, or what they have done. Recognizing a person's priceless value makes them inherently honorable, and causes us to cherish them as we would a prized possession.

Viewing someone as "honorable" causes you to treat them with holy reverence, just as you would handle material objects that are set apart for special treatment. Think of the plates your mom brings out on Thanksgiving and Christmas: you treat them honorably because they are special, compared to the paper plates you use during a barbecue and throw like a Frisbee into the trash.

In the same way, honoring someone is holding them in holy regard as special, valuable, and of immeasurable worth. The specific way to honor an individual may vary based on cultural context, but the intention is the same across all cultures.

While most people aren't consciously biased against their out-group, people could honestly conclude that they proactively demonstrate honor to others. Racism exists because people have determined, on their own and through their in-groups, who to honor and how—and, by extension, who does not make the cut.

Honoring the priceless value of the image of God in those of your out-group is a decision you make. Your choice has no correlation to whether that honor is deserved, because honoring activity is rooted in grace: undeserved favor. Dr. David A. Anderson writes in his book *Gracism: The Art of Inclusion*, "I define gracism as the positive extension of favor on other human beings based on color, class, or culture. . . . When anyone has an honor deficit . . . it is [our duty as gracists] to reach out and serve that person."

Crossing Group Lines

I recently asked Courtney to recommend a good place to eat in Boston, because I was traveling there. She referred me to her family's Italian restaurant.

That's right. Courtney is Italian. Her Black friends called her the lightest Black girl they'd ever met. She grew up as the only White girl in her housing project. She was the only White girl in her elementary school crew of Black girls. Now she lives in San Diego and has developed countless relationships with people of all races—including Mexicans, a group she once feared.

Though she looked different, they considered her part of their in-group because they chose to embrace and honor an often-overlooked in-group characteristic: that which we all share in common. That thread of commonality is what makes you, and I, and every other human, worthy of honor—the presence of God's image in us, and our membership in the human race.

Next Steps

1. Can you give examples of the three expressions of racism in your personal life?
2. Identify three ways you favor your racial in-group.

3. The next time you encounter someone from your racial out-group, take a moment to assess how much out-group discrimination you are inclined to express, and practice reversing your treatment of them.

Prayer

"Teach me to do Your will, For You are my God; Your Spirit is good. Lead me in the land of uprightness." (Psalm 143:10)

Lord, I don't have racism figured out in my own heart, but I do know that I am responsible for my thoughts, my actions, and my attitude toward others. Reveal to me the biases I have in favor of the members of my in-group. Reveal the biases I have against the members of my out-group. Help me recognize racism when I see it in myself and in the world, and empower me to counter it with grace and honor. In Jesus' name I pray, Amen.

PART II

ME

Growing up a mixed-race kid in racially segregated neighborhoods, attending predominantly White schools as a Black kid, playing on diverse football teams for three decades, living in diverse neighborhoods, and pastoring a "Skittles" church have enabled me to view people through a lens that's different from most people's. Even so, I've had to challenge myself continuously to be sensitive to my own blind spots, and I hope that whatever your background is, this book will help you do the same.

Here's what's worked for the thousands of people in our church community who live this message every day: the most important person to start with is *me*. In my youth, I'd try and fail, repeatedly, to "fix" other people by attempting to help them change their hearts. And while the desire to influence others for Christ is my driving motivation in life, I've learned to recognize that the only person I can ever truly change is me. That's probably why the only form of control the Bible directs us to exercise is self-control.

I need to look at *my* heart first. As simple as it sounds, if everyone took a good look at themselves, positive change would start happening. In fact, if everyone *only* looked at themselves, we would be a lot closer to creating a world where everyone is honored.

CHAPTER 3

Unalienable Honor

"We hold these truths to be self-evident,
that all men are created equal ..."
—THE UNITED STATES DECLARATION OF INDEPENDENCE

On Saturday, August 12, 2017, hundreds of White supremacists descended on Charlottesville, Virginia, protesting the removal of Confederate statues. Chanting racial slurs, they loudly proclaimed their hatred for people of color and Jews.

The counterprotesters who gathered in response represented a diverse cross section of our country. They roundly condemned the actions and beliefs of the White supremacists. I was encouraged to see that, in addition to civil rights leaders and politicians, regular people of all races stood shoulder to shoulder, united against hatred.

Virginia governor Terry McAuliffe had a pointed message for the extremist groups that flocked to Charlottesville that day: "Go home.... You are not wanted in this great commonwealth. Shame on you."

There's a reason so many people reacted so strongly to the White supremacists and their message of hate that day: something about their hatred of "others" violated a deep-rooted recognition in us that we are called to honor one another.

Wrongs and Rights

The very same cry for justice that Americans felt in response to what happened in Charlottesville was also uttered by the more than 250,000 people who gathered in Washington, DC, in 1963 to hear the most famous civil rights speech ever delivered in the United States. But though we're all familiar with that speech, we must not forget that the "I Have a Dream" speech by Martin Luther King Jr. was a plea to the conscience of America, both society's and the government's.

Dr. King said, "In a sense, we have come to our nation's capital to cash a check. When the architects of our republic wrote the magnificent words of the Constitution and the Declaration of Independence, they were signing a promissory note to which every American was to fall heir. This note was a promise that all men, yes, black men as well as white men, would be guaranteed the unalienable rights of life, liberty, and the pursuit of happiness."

Did you catch that? The words in his last sentence?

The reason we are outraged by injustice is because we know that every person has unalienable rights to life, liberty, and the pursuit of happiness. Neither the Declaration of Independence nor Dr. King's speech created these rights—they only articulated what we all know to be true about our existence. And these truths demand that our government and we, as individual members of our society, protect them.

The civil rights movement was launched to free all Americans— Blacks, Whites, Asians, Latinos, and everyone else—from the evil and dehumanizing grip of discrimination. The movement focused on a few specific areas that needed work: equal opportunity in employment, education, and housing; the right to vote; and equal access to public facilities. It also sought to extend to African Americans the full rights of citizenship guaranteed by the Fourteenth and Fifteenth Amendments, which had been eroded by segregationist Jim Crow laws in the South.

"We hold these truths to be self-evident, that all men are created equal, that they are endowed by their Creator with certain unalienable Rights, that among these are Life, Liberty and the pursuit of Happiness." What are these self-evident truths? What does *equality* really mean? And what effect does our equality have on our view of ourselves and our treatment of others?

Equal and Unalienable

The Declaration of Independence says "all men . . . are endowed by their Creator with certain unalienable Rights . . ." *Unalienable* means "cannot be taken away or denied." *Unalienable*—a word that can be used interchangeably with *inalienable*—means that we were born with these rights.

(By the way, I dread trying to pronounce *unalienable* on Sunday mornings, and dare you to try saying it three times fast.)

The Declaration clearly states that these rights were "endowed to us by our Creator."

We didn't earn them; we didn't design them; we didn't ask for them. God simply gave them to us. These rights have been given to us forever and are a part of our human nature. Everyone was born with the desire for life, liberty, and the pursuit of happiness, because it's been knitted into our human fabric. That's what brought 250,000 people to the National Mall to hear Dr. King, and that's why these words still resonate in our hearts. Deep down, we know we are created in God's image—but we all have work to do in honoring His image in, and the rights of, others.

Life

Life is the ability to experience all that God's put on the earth for us to discover. The length of our lives vary, but the essence of living is giving and receiving the love of God. Our greatest need in life is to love and be loved. Love includes honor, patience, empathy, forgiveness, encouragement, and almost everything every human wants that is pure, noble, and good.

Liberty

From a legal standpoint, *liberty* means the right to live without unwarranted intrusion into our privacy and property.

On a relational level, *liberty* means that you're free to pursue the calling that God has placed in your heart. This freedom is accompanied by a responsibility not only to protect your own liberty but also to respect the freedom of others. When one person's liberty is threatened, everyone's is—hence our responsibility to protect our brothers' and sisters' liberty as well as our own.

The Pursuit of Happiness

During my freshman year in college, one of my football coaches had a party at his apartment for a bunch of us players. While everyone was talking and joking around, he brought me back into his office, opened his desk drawer, and pulled out an NFL contract. It was at least five legal-size pages, each a different color. When I saw it, I thought, *Ohhh, snap!* My heart started racing. I'd dreamed about getting one of those all my life.

He handed it to me, looked me in the eye, and said, "You can get one of these."

I was in a daze the rest of the night. My coach had shown me a tangible image of the dream I had in my heart, and instilled in me a belief that my dream could actually happen. This fueled my pursuit that eventually ended in my very own NFL contract a few years later.

Everyone you meet has a dream. Imagine being someone like my coach who gives others hope to pursue their dreams.

In Jeremiah 29:11, God spoke through Jeremiah, "For I know the thoughts that I think toward you, says the Lord, thoughts of peace and not of evil, to give you a future and a hope." A future and a hope. Sounds fantastic, doesn't it? There is a future God has for your life. What future purpose have you been endowed to fulfill?

This pursuit of happiness cuts through the noise of society's drama and differences. If you can help me achieve my dream, you've got my attention. The reason coaches, teachers, and mentors are heroes is because they help fulfill our dreams.

The responsibility to honor everyone's right to life, liberty, and the pursuit of happiness is not only the government's responsibility, but also the responsibility of you and me, as individuals, in our treatment of each other, whether part of our in-group or not.

Our Big Heads

The average baby's head is about 30 percent of their weight at birth, but our son's head was pushing 45 percent. He had a "rock!" (That's slang for a big head—and, no, we didn't name the church after his "rock"!)

We'd notice people doing a double take as we walked through the mall with our big-headed baby boy. His forehead was about half the size of his face. The distance from his eyes to his hairline was the same as from his chin to his eyes.

His head was the subject of many jokes and sermon illustrations, especially when I was talking about the size of the earth or boulders on a mountainside. We got a little relief from the staring when his hair started to grow out because it was curly and Afro-like, hiding the enormity of his rock.

But then I made a decision that almost cost me my marriage. When he was seven years old, I shaved his head. He looked like he belonged on *National Geographic*. You could see every undulation, bump, curve, and angle of his skull. Boy, was my wife mad about that! (By the way, when he was little, he would tap his head and say, "Dad, talk about my head." So if you're feeling a little sorry for him, it's okay. He survived emotionally and grew into a very handsome man.)

Many years later, when my son's wife became pregnant, we were all curious about whether their son would have his head (God forbid he would have a daughter with a "rock" like that!). Thank God he had a boy, whom he also named Miles. And wouldn't you know: he has the same giant head my son had. Their baby pictures look so much alike that my grandson points to photos of his father and says, "That's me!"

My son made a son in his own image.

His son looks like him.

My son is teaching him to act like him.

My son is teaching him to see the world like him.

Our image, internal and external, are part of God's design.

While playing baseball in my yard recently, my grandson yelled "Square it up! Shoulders back!" as he positioned himself to hit the ball. He kept repeating it and said, "My daddy told me to do that."

Like our earthly fathers, God made us in His image too, so we could act like Him and look like Him, though not necessarily in the traditional sense. Our God image is the invisible aspect of our being that has the ability to have a relationship with our Creator, and express His heart to the world. We look like Him by acting like Him and loving like Him.

Genesis 1:26–27 reads, "Then God said, 'Let Us make man in Our image, according to Our likeness . . .' So God created man in His *own* image; in the image of God He created him; male and female He created them."

So, to answer the question we started with—What makes us equal?—we are equals because we each possess the same image of God. The image we carry comes, part and parcel, with unalienable rights. These rights are unalienable because God's image in us cannot be removed and because He gave them to us. Nothing and nobody—no individual, no law, no community, nobody—can separate our unalienable rights from our existence.

As you might imagine, I've spoken at many funerals, honoring all kinds of people. In every single service, no matter what kind of life the person lived, loved ones acknowledge, "God knows his heart, and I'm sure he's in a better place."

(By the way, I've never had a person look down with a sad face and say, "I don't know about Uncle Bobo. He might not be up there with the Big Man but down there with the little man. That brother was a rolling stone, and he might not have made it. The Pearly Gates might have been shut when he showed up.")

My point is that, not only do most of us have a clear sense of being eternal, but most also have a very hopeful view of where we want to go.

The image of God in us projects an eternal perspective on life. This view gets stronger the longer we live, pressing in on us just before we pass. In other words, the older we get, the closer to death we are, the more reflective we become about what might be next. It is as if God is giving us a final opportunity to acknowledge His desire to see us in heaven.

When we stop looking at petty differences and consider the eternal, we can catch a glimpse of the image of God in every human being. He made us in His image so He could see Himself in us. These words, which speak to our image, are even more astounding: "Let Us make man in Our image, according to Our likeness . . ." The divine "Us," eternally in relationship, designed the earthly "us" for eternal relationship— with God and with other people.

Jesus said: "All [the world] will know that you are My disciples, if you have love for one another" (John 13:35). This love sees and honors the image of God in other human beings.

But the image of God comes with blessings *and* responsibilities. It's the living and active image of God that makes us responsible for ensuring we fulfill God's expression of love to all people. God's image can recognize itself in others. Any time we don't live up to the standard of God's love toward others, we are acting in a manner that falls beneath who we were created to be.

The Third Option requires of individuals the same thing Martin Luther King Jr. and the signers of the Declaration of Independence required of our government. It reminds us that God assigns each and every one of us the responsibility of honoring our neighbors equally. As I said at the beginning of this chapter, everything boils back down to *me*. If we could all choose the Third Option, external mechanisms—laws, policies, protest, and social movements—would be less necessary. We would joyfully honor and value others on our own accord, rather than in begrudging obedience to a law or mandate.

Image Is Everything

When the Chargers were based in San Diego, I led ten players in a weekly Bible study. One day I sat around a block of conference tables with ten Chargers, who were all wearing sweatpants and hoodies. Some were Black, some were White. Some were from the East Coast, others from the West Coast, and some were from somewhere in between.

I handed them each a worksheet designed to guide them in sharing their faith journey with their teammates. The form began with relatively simple questions: Where did you grow up? What was the environment in your childhood home like? What's your marital status? But the next questions dug deeper into their stories. What follows are the questions I asked them. As you read these, think through how you'd answer them yourself.

I believed that if I _____ *(had sex, chased money, achieved athletic success, colleges degrees, etc.), I would be happy, fulfilled, and successful.*

So, I pursued this course of action for _____ *(months, years).*

The more I _____ *(did drugs, chased money or sex, achieved success, etc.), the more I realized that it wasn't working, because I felt* _____ *(emptiness, loneliness, a sense of failure, depressed, etc.).*

If someone asked me how I was doing, I'd have to admit that my heart was _____ *(empty, dark, unfulfilled, considering suicide, etc.) and my life was* _____ *(going nowhere, lost, etc.).*

After each player filled out the form, I asked them to share their answers. To everyone's amazement, every guy had similar responses. Each wanted to be successful, liked by their friends, and viewed sexual relationships as important.

Then I asked them *why* they believed they all had similar answers. One player said it was because they were all athletes and had football in common. I suggested two more important reasons.

First, the questions were designed to apply to their lives before their time in the NFL. They were referring to needs they'd experienced since childhood—needs that shaped the careers they chose, the decisions they'd made, and the dreams they chased.

The second and most eye-opening reason had to do with a nine-year-old kid in the room. He was the son of a staff member who attended the Bible study with us.

He had filled out the questionnaire as well, and his answers were the same as the pro athletes'—except, instead of referring to drugs and women, he referred to video games and having cool friends to hang out with. At first we all laughed about it, but when we actually took some time to dig in deeper, we realized that he had the same need to be loved and valued as all the grown-ups in the room.

My point is, whether you're young or old, Latino, Black, White, or Asian, male or female, a professional football player or a nine-year-old kid, we all have the same image of God stamped on our hearts, the same desire to be honored, and the same commitment to experiencing the fullness of our unalienable rights.

God's image is the same in everyone. James 2:8–9 says: "If you keep the law found in Scripture, 'Love your neighbor as you love yourself,' you are doing right. But if you show favoritism, you sin." Loving everyone in His image is important to God, and so is treating everyone equally.

Seeing God's Image in Ourselves

My heart breaks to see so many people enslaved by a false sense of who they are. Sadly, those who miss God's image in themselves are often the people who exhibit the greatest amount of racial prejudice and hatred. I see this reality manifested most often in prisons and juvenile detention centers—two of my favorite places to visit.

During one of my regular visits to a juvenile detention center in San Diego, the staff asked me to meet with one kid in particular. I waited in one of the cells—which consisted of concrete walls, a cot, and a metal stool—until a skinny White kid walked in. Holding his head down, he barely looked at me. During our conversation, he told me he had been physically abused most of his life. He was also a proud White supremacist.

I asked him, "Who's been abusing you?"

"My dad."

"What color is your dad?"

"White."

"He's not Black, yet you hate all Black people?"

And that's when he snapped.

He suddenly started calling me the N-word, yelling curses, and telling me to get the f* out. Because the walls are made of concrete and metal, every word echoed. Everything he screamed at me bounced off surfaces of the prison for all to hear.

The next week I went back to visit the same young man. The grateful staff told me they thought they'd lost another volunteer, and I wasn't surprised. Dealing with people who do all they can to push you away isn't for everyone.

People who hurt spend a lot of energy hurting other people, and this kid was hurt. His words didn't faze me, because I'd been on the receiving end of much worse. I was there to minister to his pain—to honorably invest in the potential of God's purpose for his life. I also understood where this young man's pain came from, and recognized that it wasn't about me.

My second visit was different. I went in understanding his pain, with a commitment to love him no matter what. I chose to remember that, deep inside, he and I both wanted and were designed for the same thing: honor.

This time our visit ended differently. Before I left, we closed our conversation by praying together.

My new friend—a White Supremacist prisoner who hated his father and hated himself—is the perfect example of someone who had missed God's image in himself. It's literally impossible for people like him to see in others what they don't recognize in themselves, until they have a personal encounter with God that changes their self-perception.

The Hope of Honor

Honor is a force that's stronger than racism, and it is the posture in which we were designed to live. *Honor* can be defined as great respect, and as a verb it means thinking about and treating others with the utmost respect.

Every day, I challenge myself to grant honor to every person I meet by acknowledging the following truths:

1. Every person has an inalienable right to *life*—physical, spiritual, and emotional life, both here on this earth, and in our relationship, now and in the future, with God. It's my responsibility to do what I can to protect my life and theirs.

2. Every person has a right to freely choose their path in life—and my job is to encourage them in the direction God has for them. If I'm being an impediment to their liberty, it's on me to recognize what I'm doing and to stop doing it.

3. God has a dream for every person, and the chasing of that dream is the essence of the pursuit of happiness. My role is to encourage people in their pursuit of that dream, and if there are any barriers to the pursuit of that dream, then I must help take them down.

In other words, I not only acknowledge and honor the rights that God has given me and every other person in the world; I also recognize the responsibilities that accompany them. And those responsibilities extend beyond how I live my life into how I treat others.

My hope is that we can shift our focus away from merely avoiding saying or doing racist things, to becoming lovers of people. When we focus on honoring others as our mission in life, differences fade. Prejudice becomes a foreign concept. We begin seeing the image of God in the people we meet, and finding joy in helping others fulfill their God-given callings.

Unalienable Me

By returning to the truth of these unalienable rights, we can love and honor others the way God loves and honors them. But that's the easy part, compared to what I'm about to drop on you next. Are you ready?

The toughest question we all have to ask ourselves isn't whether we love others the way God calls us to. Rather, we need to ask whether we will honor these truths and internalize them for *ourselves*. In this context, the question becomes: Do I believe that I have the same priceless value as others, especially those of my out-group, and that I am made in God's image?

There are so many reasons for why this is the hardest question of all. Moderating behavior and resetting the "truth button" on others is one thing—but as tens of thousands of therapists will tell you, believing something for yourself is something entirely different. All the pain of unmet childhood needs and years of sorrow, disappointment, and failure send us a message that lies to us and tells us we're not worthy. Until we believe that we are, it will be impossible to love and honor ourselves, and difficult to do the same with others.

Follow the Instructions

Awhile back I bought a play set for my grandson. The first step we had to tackle was reading the instructions on how to assemble the thing. As soon I saw the instructions I said, "Oh, dang! What was I thinking? This thing has forty-two steps!"

The play set was designed by the toy company, and I'm sure it made perfect sense to them how to put the thing together, but it was all gibberish to me. I needed their instructions to tell me what to do with it. In the same manner, our God image has been endowed to us by God. We need Him to show us how to use it, value it, and honor it.

Racism is what happens when we ignore the beauty in ourselves and in others, throw away God's instructions on how to live, and make up our own rules that result in dishonoring ourselves and others. The good news is, He is more than happy to tell us how to use the inalienable rights he's endowed us with, if we'll simply ask for His help.

The unalienable image of God in you is alive. That fact doesn't change as you get older. It doesn't change when you commit a crime. It doesn't change if you're Black or White, poor or rich. Your image was given to you by your Creator, which gives you inherent value and makes everyone you meet worthy of experiencing His honor through you.

Next Steps

1. Look in the mirror and read this statement to yourself:

   "God has given me His image. It's eternal, it's alive, and it comes with responsibilities. He has also given this same image to every other person in the world. His image in me directs me to acknowledge and honor itself in every person I meet.

   "I will look for God's image in others. I will honor it as eternally valuable."

2. Identify one person of a different ethnicity and list the characteristics of the image of God in them by completing this sentence: *Just like me,* [name] *is* [adjective] *like God,* [adjective] *like God, and* [adjective] *like God.*

3. Give that person a call and tell them what you just wrote.

Prayer

Dear Lord, I ask that You reveal to us the true nature of the unalienable image that You have given us. 1 Samuel 2:30 says, "Those who honor Me I will honor, and those who despise Me shall be lightly esteemed." I want to be a person of honor, and I want to be part of a movement of honor. Holy Spirit, I can do that only if You fill my heart with the love of the Father. In Your name I pray. Amen.

CHAPTER 4

The Honor Shift

It's not good for us to be alone.

You often hear people ask, "Why can't we all just get along?" But I think the more important question is: Are *you* willing to do whatever it takes to get along with others? And, more specifically: Are you willing to do whatever it takes to love and honor your neighbors equally—regardless of their ethnicity?

Satan is the Liar, the source of all darkness and division in this world, who has convinced us to put ourselves first, focus on the seen, and ignore the unseen. He has convinced us that what we have in common is based on our physical appearances, not the unseen eternal image of God that we all possess.

Yet, even though we're all made in the image of God, we naturally focus on ourselves. And it's impossible to honor the image of God in you when I'm obsessed with me.

In order to move beyond an unhealthy preoccupation with ourselves, we need to experience a shift.

We must learn to honor the unseen in other people. But we'll never be able to appreciate someone's outward appearance, culture, language, and history, until we honor what's inside of them. That's why so many well-meaning social programs and policies ultimately fail. They focus on the seen—the outward appearance—instead of the issue that lies at the root of the problem: our hearts.

What are you holding on to more tightly than Jesus' perception and purpose for your life? In life, we often point to money, power, status, and position as the things we look to for an identity outside of Christ. But have you ever considered the possibility that you may also be clinging to your ethnicity? Many overlook how tightly our image is wrapped around how the world views us, and how we identify ourselves along racial lines.

You might not have ever thought about this before, but I suspect your ethnic identity plays a role in how you see yourself and the world outside of yourself. Recognizing this is the beginning of a shift in your heart that Jesus will help you complete.

Debbie's Despair

Debbie grew up in a predominantly African American low-income housing project in Connecticut. She and her brother, Donal, were two typical kids living with a single mom on a very tight budget. Christmas presents for their family weren't wrapped toys from the store but hand-me-down clothes dropped off in a garbage bag.

But Debbie and her brother were different from the other kids in their housing project in one way: they were the only mixed-race kids there. Deb and Donal were very light-skinned and visibly different from everyone else they saw on a daily basis. Their mom was White and their dad was Black, but he was barely involved in their lives. Debbie remembers their dad once taking her and Donal Christmas shopping—but not for them. He bought gifts for the kids of his girlfriend, and they went home empty-handed.

Debbie and Donal's light skin made them the target of ridicule and physical harassment within the Black community. It wasn't uncommon for neighbors to throw rocks through their window, causing shattered glass to fall on them while they were in their beds. When Debbie was ten years old, she jumped between her mom and a neighbor as they fought on the ground. Just before the smackdown, she could hear a woman cursing her mother, calling her a White b* as she walked toward their housing unit.

Debbie and Donal were often beat up on their way to and from elementary school. At times they even needed a police escort. Because Debbie's hair was straight, she was teased for having "White girl hair." One day a Black student was making fun of her hair. Debbie figured that if the teacher heard what was going on, the torment would end. So, with each round of teasing, Debbie repeated "What did you say?" in the hope that the other girl would say it loud enough for the teacher to hear.

After several rounds of this taunting and repeating, the teacher, who was Black, turned to Debbie and growled, "Are you deaf? She said you have White girl hair!"

At that moment, Debbie knew there was no help to be found—not even from the people in authority at the school. Debbie turned to one of the White students and asked why they didn't pick on him and he said because he was all one color.

The message to her was clear: you are Black, but not Black enough, so Blacks will mistreat you and authority figures won't protect you. This was the narrative that she brought into adulthood. And it's the same narrative that I, and so many of my mixed-race friends, have experienced at some point in our lives.

Debbie's Shift

In high school, Debbie became determined to move out of the housing project.

She got a job and bought a car. When neighbors smashed her car window, she worked overtime to get it repaired. When someone slashed the tires, which happened on more than one occasion, she bought new tires. Eventually she worked two jobs, and she never gave up.

Debbie never gave up believing that the people who treated her negatively didn't represent everyone in their race. She ended up dating an African American guy in high school. Her two favorite bosses in high school were White men who treated her with respect and trusted her with great responsibility. She wouldn't have phrased it like this at the time, but Debbie made the conscious decision to choose the Third Option, by honoring the presence of God's image in every person instead of stereotyping them. She shifted her thinking.

She eventually left those jobs, her neighborhood, and the guy she was dating, but married another Black guy: me. That's right, Debbie is my wife. I can't even imagine what would have happened to Debbie's life, and mine, if she hadn't made the shift to honor the unseen potential in people, as opposed to allowing her negative experiences to shape how she saw herself and others.

The Shift in Shaker Heights

I recently heard a fascinating story about the Shaker Heights City School District, an upper-middle-class neighborhood in Ohio.

The demographics of Shaker Heights are 55 percent White, 37 percent African American, and 8 percent Asian, but the school district's makeup is 48 percent African American and 40 percent White.[12]

What accounts for this difference? In 1983, the Student Group on Race Relations (SGORR) launched campus-wide initiatives to narrow the academic achievement gap between Black students and White students. At the time, 80 percent of the failing grades were received by

African American students, even though they came from families with similar income levels as their White classmates.

Teachers and parents wondered why Black students from similar socioeconomic backgrounds and the same neighborhood who attended the same school didn't do as well as White students.

What they observed was that the African American, White, Latino, and Asian kids were all friends throughout elementary school. But when they reached seventh and eighth grade, they started to develop identities based on their race. African American kids started hanging out with kids who looked like them. White kids gravitated to other White kids. Why? Because the easiest way to connect with "people like me" is based on what I see: skin color. It's the most obvious in-group we have.

When SGORR launched, its founding students could see that this racial divide not only changed friendship circles in junior high; it also influenced the composition of advanced placement classes, the colleges to which students applied, and the careers different groups aspired to have.

SGORR set out to address the racial divide in Shaker Heights schools, and continues to do so three decades later. Each year more than three hundred high school students learn how to become SGORR facilitators. Mixed-race high school teams visit fourth- and sixth-grade classrooms to teach these younger students about peer pressure, stereotyping, and problem solving. The impact of the program is seen in how interracial friendships are preserved, and academic trajectories remain on track, irrespective of race.[13]

Who and How

In our teens, we become conscious of *who* we are and *how* we identify ourselves. We naturally identify with people who look like us, and groups are formed. Once you're in a group, the belief system of that group is formed and reinforced: *Hey, what are you doing wearing those preppy clothes? Why are you using that hip-hop slang? Why are you listening to that White music?*

Once the Shaker Heights City School District staff identified a root cause of school disengagement, they developed a mentoring program in which older kids helped younger students focus on common goals and question stereotypes. As a result, there was a drastic increase in the number of African American students taking AP classes, moving on to college, and getting better careers.

An identity that's primarily based on the visible is dangerous. Skin color and culture are certainly a part of our identity, as we'll discuss in another chapter, but the image of God that connects us is invisible and more powerful.

The Honor Shift

During a recent staff meeting at my church, we asked everyone to form groups with those who didn't look like them, and answer three questions. About 140 of our staff were in attendance, and they're as diverse as our congregation, which is one of the most diverse congregations in America.

The first question was: When was the first time you were aware of your ethnicity? Often people will remember an incident when someone called them a name, or a time their parents told them about their culture, or a story of discrimination.

I remember being in the first grade, sitting in class, and looking around thinking, *No one here looks like me.* I felt out of place and I knew I was different.

The second question was: What were you told by your family about people of other ethnic groups?

I was told by the actions of my family to treat everyone with respect. After all, one of my grandmothers was White, and the other was Black and Chinese. This was exemplified in the diversity of relationships that my parents and relatives enjoyed. However, growing up in the 1960s and '70s—the height of the civil rights era—I learned through television and my life experiences that Whites were in control of America's power structures—including the government, the media, and corporate America—and that they had a negative, condescending view of African Americans. Minorities were rarely portrayed as being in positions of influence and power, and had to fight for their rights.

The third question was: How did it make you feel to share these answers with your group today, and how did their answers affect you?

Telling my story made me think about how my early experiences still impact my views today. Sometimes, we don't know what we really feel until we verbally express it. As Scripture says, "What we say flows from what is in our hearts" (Luke 6:45).

The questions above help inform us of how our "social narrative" was formed. Our social narrative is the story we believe about who we are, how we are to be, and how we want to be known. It's also the story about who we think everyone else is and how we think they will *likely* act toward us.

Our story dictates everything about the way we view ourselves and others. We rely on our social narrative to inform us of how others might treat us and how we should respond. This is all an attempt to protect the identity we've created for ourselves, or the identity that's been created for us—which may be one and the same.

Who I am has been shaped by stories I've been told about me and those like me, as well as through my personal experiences. Unfortunately, our identity is often shaped by a flawed and biased social narrative, and even our own hearts lie to us about who we really are.

But as we discussed in the previous chapter, the image God placed in you is the strongest influence on your true identity. Your visible image is part of your identity, but only a small part. Our tendency is not to honor God's image inside of us but to put our culture, color, and story first. Our task, then, is to shift the way we think by choosing the Third Option, so as to purposefully honor the image of God in every person starting with ourselves. This is what I call the "Honor Shift."

Let's be honest: it's so much easier to identify with others based on outward appearances and in-group biases. But God wants to shift us out of what's easy and into what pleases Him and, ultimately, brings peace to us.

A Moment of Self-Reflection

When was the first time you became acutely aware of your race? Was it a bad experience? Was it something your parents told you, something some kid said at school, or something you saw on TV or the Internet?

I'm sure there are several experiences that shaped the way you view yourself, as well as your own race and other races. Share these with someone you trust, listen to yourself talk, and you'll begin to understand what your heart feels about yourself and about other people.

How does it feel when you hear yourself answer the above questions? Do you have more biases in your heart than you thought? If so, welcome to the human race. You are not alone in this journey, and I'm here to help you make the shift.

Most important, how do these feelings and perceptions line up with your God-given responsibility to honor His image in others?

Until we're in mutually honoring, interdependent, and loving relationships with "others," we won't be living up to our God-given potential. The minute we begin to think life is all about *us*, that's when we dishonor our purpose and dishonor those around us.

Is it time for a shift in your heart?

The Bigger Story

We're all part of a picture that's much larger than any one person, like individual tiles in a mosaic. The big picture is designed to accomplish something no one person alone can accomplish. We must all work together to create a society that's genuinely peaceful and unified. But doing so requires an honor shift that starts with each individual.

Consider how beautiful a multicolored bouquet of flowers can be. Besides the variety of colors and flowers, the bouquet produces a unified and unique scent. No one, two, or even three flowers alone could create a scent the bouquet gives off as a whole. This beautiful aroma requires the combination of all the flowers.

Similarly, our social circles should honor the unique human bouquet of color and culture that reflects the full glory of God. We must learn to honor not just the seen but also the unseen. We must learn to focus not just on the here and now but on the eternal purpose and potential that's been endowed to us.

Ephesians 2:10 says, "For we are His workmanship, created in Christ Jesus for good works, which God prepared beforehand that we should walk in them."

With the love the Father had for His son, we were given life and a purpose. We can only fulfill this purpose within the context of the greater mosaic of humanity.

How does your social narrative affect your ability to play the role that only you can play in the mosaic of life? What did God put you on this earth to do, at this very specific moment in time, looking just like you do, with the experiences you've had?

If you don't play your role properly and bring your unique tile to the picture, the mosaic won't be complete. We need you in the picture.

Ultimately, you have been given free will, and you get to decide for yourself whether you want to be part of the bigger picture. It's your choice. But in order to get there, you might have to question the stories you've been told about who you are and who other people are. It isn't always easy, but God will help you through the process.

There's a version of yourself that God has endowed you with—one in which love overcomes hate, freeing you to pursue your dreams without the hindrance of internal and external pressures to conform to what others think you should be.

There's an unseen part of us that, if embraced, will make us better people and allow us to build a better society. We'll have more friends, more peace, and more opportunities than we could imagine.

As the unseen comes together, we begin to see the full picture, no longer as thousands of small tiles, but as one unified image. That image is a reflection of the heart of our loving God Himself.

Next Steps

Discuss these three questions with a friend:

1. Describe the first time you were aware of your race.

2. What were you told about people of another ethnic group while growing up?

3. How did it make you feel to share these answers with your friend today, and how did their answers affect you?

Prayer

"Open my eyes, that I may see Wondrous things from Your law." (Psalm 119:18)

Dear Lord, open the eyes of my heart that I may accept the necessary changes that I need to make. Open the eyes of my heart that I may see the flaws in my social narrative, the story I've come to believe that defines who I am. I pray this in Your holy name, Amen.

CHAPTER 5

Blind Spots

I'm not racist; I have a [*ethnic group*] *friend.*

A workplace diversity consultant recently told me about a meeting she had with a school principal who expressed his deep commitment to creating an inclusive and racially diverse workplace. To introduce the consultant, the principal proudly invited his staff into the meeting room.

Every employee was Latino, just like him.

This principal's intent did not match his impact. In other words, what he described as his stated desire didn't match the actual result. That is what it means to have a "blind spot."

We're all guilty of this on some level.

Most people in the United States would say they are not racist. In fact, when asked, a clear majority of citizens would say they love and respect people regardless of race. So, what explains the racial divide that still persists in this country? A blind spot! There's a disconnect between intention and reality. I applaud intention, but without an aligned reality, intention falls short of the goal.

If you want to ensure that your intent to love those of a different race is matched by reality—what you do, say, and think—then you've got to start identifying your blind spots. Only after you identify what your blind spots are can you address and correct them.

Everyone Has Blind Spots

We all have blind spots when it comes to race. Many of us are defensive about them when they're pointed out to us. But this reaction misses the point. This is due to the fact that when culture asks "Are you a racist?" there are only two answers you can give: yes or no. Culture doesn't ask what your blind spots are, so most answer no, without any further intro-spection or discussion.

Culture also makes us jump to conclusions about others by asking, "Are THEY racist?" Since we're generally less gracious with others, we're more likely to label them as racists. Not knowing or understanding what's in another's heart causes us to make assumptions based on their words and actions, leading to judgment, shame, and broken relation-ships between accusers and the accused.

Culture leads us to dead-end conversations that get us nowhere fast. The Third Option, however, frees us from culture's trap by ex-posing our blind spots so that we can focus on who God wants us to become. The Third Option acknowledges that we are flawed with blind spots while giving us the opportunity to correct them.

The truth is, all of us have blind spots, whether we acknowledge them or not.

A blind spot doesn't mean you don't *want* to see something; it means you *can't* see what you're missing. Just like blind spots pose a danger for drivers, blind spots also pose a danger in your relationships.

How do we get around these blind spots in our natural line of vi-sion? By turning our heads so that we can get a full and accurate field of vision around us. I never wanted to "offend" a mailbox with my car, but all my good intentions didn't keep me from knocking one over as I backed out of my friend's driveway. Blind spots can be dangerous, but by turning our heads we can get a good, clear, and accurate perception of reality.

Every time we open our eyes, light enters our pupils and shines onto our retinas. Inside our retinas are millions of photoreceptors: nerve cells that interpret light and transmit the information to the brain. Every human being has small areas on their retinas where there are no photoreceptors. Medically speaking, these are known as blind spots.

If you want to "see" one of your blind spots in action, I have an easy exercise for you. Look at the diagram below from about two feet away, with your right eye closed. Focus on the "+" with your left eye and slowly move the image closer. At one point you'll see the dot becomes invisible. This shows the blind spot in your retina.

Based on limitations in our physiology, our brains routinely fill in gaps that our eyes don't see. And just as our brains fill those blind spots in our eyes, we also fill in our relational blind spots based on our past experiences, good and bad.

While we may *think* we can see everything clearly, what we actually see before us may, in fact, be a blind spot, backfilled by our brains. It's human nature to project what we *expect* to see, rather than rewrite the script we've followed all our lives.

This is especially true when describing people who are part of our out-group. Remember, this is a group we don't have accurate information about because of our limited exposure to them. As a result, we generalize and use stereotypes to fill in the blanks where our real knowledge is lacking.

Because of our blind spots, we often stereotype others by assuming that a member of some group, such as a racial group different than our own, has certain characteristics, without having relevant information about them. All we know is what we've seen and experienced in our limited interactions with them. But because we *aren't* them, or part of their group, we're really only filling in our blind spots with what we *think* we know.

Dr. Zachary Green, a professor of practice in leadership studies at the University of San Diego, refers to this blind spot as the gap between our "espoused theory" and "theory in use." His perspectives are based on the work of organizational theorist Chris Argyris.

Your "espoused theory" is what you claim to believe about someone or something. Your "theory in use" is the actual behavior you exhibit. Even though the difference between the two is sometimes intentional, often it's not.

The reason for this gap is twofold: (1) our own social narrative, and (2) social reinforcement that reinforces the beliefs that we have come to learn. We continue to tell ourselves the truths that have come to define not only who we are but who everyone else is. When you surround yourself with people who hold the same beliefs you do, there is little room to expand your understanding of how others experience the world. Our social narrative is strongly influenced by our family, friends, classmates, and neighbors.

Social Narratives

When Dena was eleven years old, her Iraqi family, who had previously moved from Baghdad to Detroit, relocated to San Diego.

Throughout her life, whenever guys asked about her cultural origins and she admitted to being from Iraq, they mysteriously lost interest in her.

To counter this, Dena learned to lie about her ethnicity. She pretended to be more acceptable as a date by faking Italian and Greek heritage. She even changed the pronunciation of her last name to sound more American.

One summer afternoon, while Dena was swimming in a friend's pool, her hair, which she purposely kept straight to conceal her ethnicity, suddenly went curly. A guy who didn't know her all that well said, "Hey, you have curly hair!" Before Dena could respond, her best friend—a blonde with whom she did everything—replied, "All Iraqi girls have curly hair." Everyone else was shocked: they had had no idea Dena was from Iraq.

This opened up a whole new conversation about their preconceived assumptions of Iraqi women. They asked questions like "How are you even allowed to hang out with us? Aren't Middle Eastern women prohibited from leaving the house? Going to college? Talking to guys outside of their own culture?"

Her first response was "Have you ever met a Middle Eastern person?" To which they replied, "No!"

She explained to them that she had the same freedoms and aspirations as they did. She said she planned to go to college and do everything this country afforded her the opportunity to do, and that her family and culture supported her. Their assumptions were based solely on hearsay and not firsthand experience or knowledge. She was part of an out-group they knew very little about. She eventually dated one of those guys, and today she is still friends with many of those whom she educated that afternoon.

We get our primary identity from our parents and from our early childhood experiences. It's human nature to focus on the outward appearance of others, and therefore to shine light on one of the visible differences that exists between races. But as we've already discussed, the unseen is most important to God. "Man looks at the outward appearance, but the Lord looks at the heart" (1 Samuel 16:7).

Our early experiences form not only our racial identities but a definition of who falls into "the other" categories. Every experience we have, and every story we're told about "others," projects an identity and an anticipated behavior or response onto them.

Some see a teenage Black male and immediately fear for their safety. Others may stereotype all Latinas as hot-tempered. Many will see White kids and think they are all privileged with wealth. These stereotypes stem from memories, conversations, and subconscious messages we've processed over the years. This social narrative fills in blanks, but only partially, and usually incorrectly.

If I asked what your general impressions were of people of another race, your brain would begin to review all the positive and negative "footage" you've accumulated and form a conclusion.

I went to a gathering where most people were of that race and hated it.

A stranger of that race helped me with my car one day.

I was cursed out by one of them.

My babysitter was this race and she was so wonderful.

My mother was fired by one of them.

A coworker of that race helped me get the promotion.

This is how blind spots are formed. We project our assumptions of what others are like, based on past experiences. And usually we let the experiences that had the greatest impact on us shape our perceptions of "those people" as a whole.

Every single one of us has stories that have shaped our views of others based on their races. So if we're going to commit ourselves to honoring others, we must address our blind spots. Once we recognize them, we can decide to "turn our heads" and challenge the flawed assumptions we hold in our hearts.

Unconscious Preference in America

In their book *Blindspot: Hidden Biases of Good People*, psychologists Mahzarin R. Banaji and Anthony G. Greenwald explore the hidden biases we all carry from a lifetime of exposure to cultural attitudes about age, gender, race, ethnicity, religion, social class, sexuality, disability status, and nationality. Banaji and Greenwald study the extent to which our perceptions of social groups subconsciously shape our likes and dislikes and our judgments about people's character, abilities, and potential.[14]

Their book assesses our hidden biases based on the results of over fourteen million people who took the Implicit Association Test. The Implicit Association Test is an online exercise that tests the people's attitudes—primarily their positive and negative associations—regarding certain groups of people. The data they've collected is revealing, and shows a clear disconnect between what "good people" believe about themselves and what their answers actually reveal. Here's a link to the test if you're interested in learning more about your own blind spots: https://implicit.harvard.edu/implicit/user /agg/blindspot/indexrk.htm.

This fascinating book reveals that in America the preference for White people is pervasive. The authors point to studies in which people with higher levels of preference for Whites judged White job applicants to be better qualified than Black applicants. Another study showed that emergency room physicians more often recommended optimal treatment options to White patients than to Black patients.

While both studies refer to the preference for White people over Black, the authors cite numerous examples of how "unconscious cognition" negatively affects the treatment of Latinos, Asians, Muslims, and Native Americans as well.

Making Brain Waves

Biased perspectives are formed throughout our childhood, and manifest themselves more fully in our middle school years.[15] These impressions, which shape our perspectives of others, are stored in the amygdala, located deep within the brain—the same part of the brain that controls memory, fear, and threat.[16]

Our brain is naturally designed to group things together to make sense of the world for us. The brain quickly categorizes all the information it's bombarded with and "tags" it with general descriptions the way a mail handler would quickly sort a pile of letters according to their zip codes. These experiences and associated tags play a role in forming our social narrative and how we see other people. We then apply labels such as "good" or "bad" to entire groups. When we encounter "bad" people, the amygdala kicks in to warn and protect us.

Numerous studies have shown that, among both Caucasian *and* African American observers, seeing an individual with darker skin and more Afro-ethnic features (kinkier hair, broader nose, and fuller lips) prompted more amygdala warning activity in the brain. As the observer viewed lighter faces with more Eurocentric features, their amygdala's responses decreased.

Worth noting, however, is the fact that although African American perceivers also had an increased amygdala response to darker skin and more Afrocentric features, their amygdalae reacted less dramatically than Caucasians'. In other words, seeing dark-skinned people caused both groups to react with fear, but Black people had less of a fear reaction in their brains than White people did in theirs.

Our brain works to typecast people so quickly that our conscious mind isn't even aware of what it's doing. Thankfully, we can retrain our brain—or at least become more aware of its reactions. I cannot tell you how many times, while getting into shape to play football, I had to retrain my brain to stop telling me to cut my runs short because my body was tired. Over time it adjusted its view of pain. So the question really becomes: Are you willing to "be transformed by the renewing of your mind" (Romans 12:2) or "discipline [your] body and bring it into subjection" (1 Corinthians 9:27) to the point that it can reject any dishonoring response?

Rejecting Biases

Every preconceived bias you have about a people group you're unfamiliar with originates in your culture, environment, or upbringing.

Numerous studies have proven the impact of media-enforced racial stereotypes on American culture. For example, a recent study of the Los Angeles media market found that 37 percent of the suspects portrayed in television news stories about crime were Black, although Blacks made up only 21 percent of those arrested in the city.[17] Another study found that Whites represented 35 percent of homicide victims in the local news, but only 13 percent of homicide victims in crime reports.[18] And while only 10 percent of victims in crime reports were Whites who had been victimized by Blacks, these crimes made up 42 percent of televised cases.[19] These are but a sampling of many studies that have led researchers to conclude that biases in media coverage "distort the public's sense of who commits crime," and "trigger racially biased reactions" among viewers.[20] The media literally has the power to shape an entire generation's perception of a racial group. However, being aware of the media's influence on our culture helps us filter what we see through a more critical lens.[21]

Social reinforcement—from family members, peers, and society at large—further amplifies our biases. One example of this is the globally standardized Western ideal of beauty—light skin, straight hair, and light eyes—which excludes most people of color. Even our Western portrayals of Jesus as green-eyed and light-skinned reinforces our association of European features with goodness and love versus his Middle Eastern heritage.

Many of us are affected by these social and cultural influences, because that's how we were raised. But God wants us to buy into His truth instead: that every person—regardless of the color of their skin, the texture of their hair, the color of their eyes, or any other physical traits they possess—is equally worthy of our love.

As Christians, we must vigorously reject the lie of "idealized standards," recognizing that it originates in our fallen culture and runs counter to God's truth. As we train ourselves to look past outward appearances, we'll begin to honor the hearts—rather than the skin tones—of our brothers and sisters. Then, and only then, can true racial reconciliation begin.

Recognizing Your Blind Spots

In the movie *Remember the Titans*, several football players are walking down the street together when Sunshine, a White player, suggests going into a particular bar. Petey and Blue, both Black players, are hesitant, and Petey says it isn't a good idea.

Sunshine is convinced they are overreacting. Before they know it, the stone-faced manager affirms Petey's fears. They are asked to leave. Sunshine was blind to the strong prejudices the others players know all too well.

Furious and embarrassed, Petey tells Sunshine that he warned him this would happen. Blue, in an attempt to defend Sunshine, says, "He didn't know." Petey shoots back, "He didn't *want* to know."

Recognizing your blind spots is a critical element of embracing the Third Option. Do *you* want to know what *your* blind spots are?

If so, the first step in discovering your blind spots is being willing to admit they exist. What can be more honorable than looking at yourself in the mirror and asking, *Is there something I'm not seeing about myself or my perception of others that's racially offensive?*

"And why do you look at the speck in your brother's eye, but do not consider the plank in your own eye? Or how can you say to your brother, 'Let me remove the speck from your eye'; and look, a plank is in your own eye? Hypocrite! First remove the plank from your own eye, and then you will see clearly to remove the speck from your brother's eye" (Matthew 7:3–5).

Why is it important to recognize our blind spots? Because it's a necessary part of our personal growth. Identifying our blind spots and understanding why they exist increase our self-awareness. Developing more self-awareness puts us in better alignment with who we are meant to be. This, in turn, allows us to have a greater sensitivity toward and awareness of others, especially members of our out-group.

When you're oblivious to your own blind spots, they become invisible boundaries, limiting your ability to connect with others. But if you're willing to humble yourself and ask God to reveal your blind spots, you'll be empowered to overcome them.

One More Thing . . .

Those who feel the effects of your blind spots are not nearly as blind to them as you are.

In other words, you may not see how your actions are offensive, but others not only see them, they *feel* them. Sometimes they communicate them to you in the form of criticism, advice, frustration, or anger—occasionally, perhaps a gentle rebuff—but no matter how the insight comes, I urge you to open your heart and ask God to help you receive it.

For those who've been offended, I offer the following encouragement: God knows your pain and wants to be the One who encourages you.

But more important, He wants to turn that which is intended to hurt you into something that can make you stronger.

"My brethren, count it all joy when you fall into various trials, knowing that the testing of your faith produces patience. But let patience have its perfect work, that you may be perfect and complete, lacking nothing" (James 1:2–4).

Ask Him to reveal the lessons you need to learn with each incident.

Next Steps

1. True or false: *I believe that I have racial blind spots.* Before answering this, consider taking the Implicit Association Test on page 63.

2. What friend is most equipped to reveal your racial blind spots to you?

3. Ask them what they are.

Prayer

Jesus prayed for a blind man, and something surprising happened:

> "He [Jesus] *asked him if he saw anything. And he looked up and said, 'I see men like trees, walking.' Then He put His hands on his eyes again and made him look up. And he was restored and saw everyone clearly."* (Mark 8:23–25)

> *Lord, just as you prayed for the blind man more than once, we know that bringing light to our blind spots will take time. Help me to see how I might be unintentionally offensive and give me the courage to humble myself under the loving direction of the Holy Spirit. Reveal to me how I can be more honoring of Your love and purpose in the lives of others, no matter what they look like. I pray this in Jesus' name. Amen.*

CHAPTER 6

Blind Spots in Action

"Believe me, I'm not racist, but..."

Since blind spots imply... well, blindness, I figured it would be helpful to call a few out. There are hundreds of potential blind spots to explore, but the nine outlined below seem to be the most common.

Before we dive in, let's do a gut check—or heart check. Because you're reading this, I know you're motivated to grow and change. But without one essential ingredient, your growth will be limited. That essential ingredient is humility.

Before destruction the heart of a man is haughty,
And before honor is humility. (Proverbs 18:12)

Before we can honor others, or receive honor ourselves, we must be willing to humble our hearts before God. Humility isn't thinking less *of* ourselves but thinking less *about* ourselves and more about others. This is impossible without God, because our sinful human nature will always fight to regain its rightful place at the center of ourselves. But with God, all things are possible, including humility.

Pray that God would reveal any lack of humility that arises—often in the form of defensiveness—as we explore these common blind spots. Ask God to reveal how any of these blind spots may apply to you.

If any do apply to you, they've likely been part of your story for many years. They may seem impossible to overcome, but God has promised to help you along the way.

Nine Blind Spots

1 *I claim that I don't have a racist bone in my body, but resist letting certain people get too close to my family.*

I received a call from a friend, asking for me to meet with him and his wife. They're a nice middle-class White couple, but were very vague about what they wanted to discuss.

We met for dinner, and they started to explain how they grew up in a White neighborhood and didn't have a racist bone in their bodies. *Ahhh! I've seen this movie before.*

They took a deep breath and finally got to the point. Their teenage daughter was dating a Black guy. "What do you think about that, Miles?"

If there's such a thing as an *Oh, my goooooooodness* smile, I was wearing it. "Well, the first thing that comes to my mind is, you never invited me to dinner to ask about her dating White guys!"

When you claim that racism is a nonissue but become concerned about one of your children dating or hanging with friends of your out-group, you have a blind spot. Or, as Jeff Foxworthy might say: "If you love all people, as long as they all don't live on your street . . . you might have a blind spot." Is there an out-group that would make you react like this family?

2 *I claim all people are equal, but in my heart I believe that my ethnicity is superior to others.*

This one is really subtle, but it speaks volumes about what you really think about your friends. Here's an example of how it might play out in your life.

You have a friend who's of a different ethnicity, and you always invite them into your world, but you show no interest, never ask to be invited, nor accept any invitation to participate in theirs. You pretend to feel equal with them, but secretly you think that what you have to offer them is better than anything they can offer you.

You call them your friend and your equal, but in your mind, you are their helper, savior, and safe haven.

Because of your sense of superiority, you feel that there is nothing to learn from them, and no benefit to entering into their world. Their family has nothing to offer you and your family. You would not be comfortable in their world, and you have no interest in it. You view yourself as having the sole responsibility and ability to be the giver, the teacher, and the director, rather than the student or recipient of help. You insist on events happening on your turf and on your terms.

If this is your blind spot, turn things around by giving your friend the freedom to plan and lead your next time together. Ask to enter their world, and give yourself the opportunity to learn and receive from them.

Sidenote: Have you made any assumptions about what the two people and the neighborhoods in this story look like? What are those assumptions based on?

3 *I claim all people are equal, but I feel and act inferior to certain people because I have internalized the views of my critics.*

I was walking into a high school and heard a group of guys listening to music that was using racially derogatory terms. The music also described the stereotypical limitations and negative behavior that come along with those terms. Then I heard the guys referring to each other by the same names used in the music, and heard them talking about things they couldn't do because of that identification. As I walked by, I did not see Black and Latino guys with any limitations. I saw a young teacher, a businessperson, a doctor, a lawyer. I wished that they saw themselves that way, too. I wished there was no room for those negative thoughts and self-perceptions to exist in their own minds.

This blind spot causes you to resent others who characterize you as "less than," but you unconsciously adopt those negative characterizations and reinforce those negative expectations in how you think about yourself and others like you.

When culture constantly sends a message that people like you are not favored, you can internalize that message and become imprisoned in the inferior description of your critics. A telltale sign that this is happening is that you adopt the label of your critics and reinforce the beliefs about what you "cannot" do or become, because according to your critics, you are inferior. Additionally you might find yourself doubting your ability to be all God has said you can be, simply because labels that others have placed on you have become more real to you than the destiny God has placed on you.

This self-hate or racial cannibalism is a form of internalized racism. As Scripture says, "Death and life are in the power of the tongue, and those who love it will eat its fruit" (Proverbs 18:21).

In order to stop this form of racism in its tracks, we must think on and say things that are honorable, pure, holy, and in line with how God sees you.

Say to yourself, out loud:

I am made in the image of God and not my critics. I am created to reflect the glory of God—not the limitations of man.

I will only speak honorably about myself and everyone else.

4 *I resent being the victim of discrimination and stereotyping, but have no problem doing it to others.*

In pursuit of her associate's degree in political science, Rachel walked into the counselor's office with a letter of recommendation from her college professor, endorsing her for an advanced English class on critical thinking. Rachel wanted to challenge herself by taking this class.

The counselor, noticing her Spanish accent, asked if Rachel was a native English speaker. She had come to this country from Mexico as a freshman in high school, speaking no English, but transitioned out of ESL (English as Second Language) in two years.

She wondered what his question had to do with anything, but she answered, "No, I'm originally from Mexico."

The counselor proceeded to give his reasons for denying her application, stating that the class would be too difficult for her and that she wouldn't be able to keep up with the work. Students were required to have a B in the basic English class to qualify for the advanced class. Rachel was an A student with a 3.5 GPA. But what really offended her the most was that this counselor, who was also Latino, was holding her accent against her.

Do you, like the counselor—whose own self-limiting beliefs limited others—have a blind spot that causes you to treat others in the same ways you've suffered from mistreatment?

If you find yourself attacking others, the first thing you need to ask yourself is: *Is it possible I'm insecure about something?* You cannot pull someone down unless you feel like you are below them. You were made in God's image to represent Him as a comforter to the fainthearted, an upholder of the weak, and an encourager to the discouraged. So focus on being only someone who builds people up—and that includes building yourself up as well.

5 *I claim all people are God's children, but treat some like they belong to another family.*

Esli, a twenty-five-year-old Mexican woman and worship leader in a predominantly White church, approached her pastor with an idea for a citywide youth outreach that would include a well-known guest speaker. The pastor dismissed the idea, reminding her that the church's community, who were mostly White ranchers, would never financially support her because she was a Mexican woman. "Ministry like that is not done by Mexican women, only men."

John, a White member of the church who had recently been released from prison, heard of the idea and encouraged Esli to pursue it. She told him about being rejected by the pastor, but John persisted. He invited her to come to a coalition of pastors meeting and present her idea.

During her presentation, none of the pastors looked at her except the pastor she'd originally spoken to, who was visibly angry. Everyone else was talking with each other or checking their phones. When John began to speak, they all lifted their heads to listen, and eventually agreed to support the event. As a result, three thousand young people from sixteen schools attended the outreach, and hundreds dedicated their lives to God.

The blind spot Esli's pastor and the coalition of pastors suffer from is common. How often do we dismiss people because they don't look like people who we generally recognize as those in authority? When Saul was looking to anoint the next king in Israel, he went to Jesse's home and asked him to bring out his sons. After evaluating all seven of his tall, good-looking sons, God said that none of them qualified. He then asked Jesse if he had any other sons. Jesse did not even consider his youngest, David, who was out taking care of the sheep. Once he brought him in front of Saul, God confirmed that he was the one. That little kid David became Israel's greatest king. God does not look at a person's outward appearance but at their heart.

Esli now oversees a ministry at our church that is larger than the entire church where she previously served. But blind spots prevented the pastors from seeing the anointing of her life, and almost kept the church from blessing the youth in their community.

6 *I claim to acknowledge many perspectives in life, but I'm not really willing to learn from any views that challenge mine.*

You've heard the expression, "We judge ourselves by our intent, but judge others by their actions." The truth is, we're not in a position to judge either. When we believe our intuition is flawless, we quickly judge that someone else is being biased toward us, when in fact the only bias on display is our own. Honoring others involves treating every single encounter as a separate situation, and having a willingness to listen and learn from each person individually.

Those who are doing well in life often view society through the lens of a "just-world bias." This is defined as the tendency for people to assume that the world is just and that therefore people get what they deserve in life. Just-world bias presumes that bad things happen to people who make bad choices, while good things happen to people who make good choices. It doesn't take into account an individual's personal story or a people's collective history, which is a critical element in understanding—not *defending* but *understanding*—why people feel or act the way they do.

No one would argue that hard work and doing the right thing yield positive results in life. However, when you know and love people who were born into challenging situations that continue to smack them in the face, your heart starts to challenge this view of the world. When you see obstacles keep popping up for some people that wouldn't exist for others, causing them to give up in despair, it is difficult to simply chalk their failure up to their own fault.

When you see people suffering from hardship, this blind spot will cause you to believe they must have made bad choices in life, and therefore they must be getting what they deserve. My challenge to you is to ask God to help you see other factors that may have contributed to their hardship.

Romans 8:37 says, "Yet in all these things we are more than conquerors through Him who loved us." If this is true, your recognition of what appears to be failure in someone else's situation may be your cue to help them overcome their obstacles.

When you recognize that God doesn't make losers and begin seeing each person you meet as someone with the potential to win, you start winning the battle against this blind spot. Not only will you start seeing the full truth of another's experience, you may also start to ask how you can help bring out the winner God created that person to be.

7 *I'm an unintentional participant in a bigoted system, so I am insulated from the guilt of the bigotry.*

By now it's possible that you realize how your social narrative has shaped a flawed understanding of certain people, including those who look like you.

It's also possible that you are watching news channels, listening to talk radio shows, or engaging in social media feeds that reinforce biased views. You may also be aware that everyone has an agenda not only to inform but to influence your opinion, because division equates to an uptick in ratings.

This blind spot shields you from recognizing that you are supporting the biased garbage you consume. It also absolves you from recognizing that you are complicit in the bigoted intentions of those sources.

Here's a better way to approach media consumption: Ask yourself if what you're watching or listening to helps or hinders your ability to love your neighbor. Does it make you feel more justified in your biases, or does it foster a sense of compassion in your heart?

You get to choose what you fill your mind with. Choose to fill it with information that builds up people rather than tears them down. Don't make it harder on yourself to love your neighbor. Challenge information that causes division and cut ties to any influence that dishonors, rather than honors, your neighbor.

Matthew 5:29: "If your right eye causes you to stumble, gouge it out and throw it away. It is better for you to lose one part of your body than for your whole body to be thrown into hell."

8 *I claim that because racism doesn't impact me, it doesn't exist— or at least to the degree that people say it does.*

The Stephenses, a White couple preparing to adopt a Black child, asked for advice from the Wrights, an African American couple. The Wrights, who lived in the same neighborhood, asked if they were ready to deal with the racist pushback they'd be sure to face as a result of their decision to adopt a Black child. With a bewildered, almost offended look on their faces, the adopting couple said, "We aren't racists, and racism is not part of our lives. We are going to love this child just like we love our other kids."

The Stephenses truly believed that because they were not racist, and because they had never experienced racism themselves, racism didn't exist the way the Wrights knew it did. It wasn't until they actually began raising their child that they experienced the racism they'd been warned about—racism that had previously lain dormant in the hearts of certain family members, neighbors, friends, and students in their local school. It wasn't until they welcomed their new addition to the family that they encountered a covert hatred that had found its target: their adopted Black son.

In this day and age, we'd be hard-pressed to find someone who does not believe that racism exists at all. But I meet a lot of people who dismiss or minimize racism's impact on certain groups of people, often sincerely, though sometimes purposefully—especially if acknowledging it requires them to make changes to their own worldviews or actions.

I know how difficult it is to wrap your mind around something that you have little or no experience dealing with. That's why this blind spot often dismisses people who are affected by racism as "exaggerators," which magnifies its damaging effects.

Unfortunately, some who are affected by this blind spot turn a deaf ear and a mute tongue to opportunities for dialogue and empathy. You'll often hear them say things like *Why can't you just get over it?* accompanied by *Puh-leeze* and an eye roll. Their underlying belief is that racism is not really *that* much of an issue from their perspective, so it can't *possibly* be that much of an issue in someone else's life.

It's one thing to confront the challenges of everyday life when everyone looks like you and gives you the benefit of the doubt. It's an entirely different thing to feel unheard, ignored, or mocked about your experiences with racism as a member of an out-group. Ultimately, before responding, the onus is on each and every one of us to hear our brothers and sisters out—and to pray for the Holy Spirit's guidance in understanding their grievances.

9 *I don't have any blind spots. I see things just fine.*

All I have to say is: *Nice to meet you, Jesus.*

Seriously, we've all had this thought at one time or another. But some have adopted it as a lifestyle. We're all suffering from a *blind spot bias.* This is the tendency to see oneself as less biased than most other people, or the failure to see the impact of biases on one's own judgments and evaluations.

This is exactly what pride wants you to believe: that you're not part of the problem. But the reality is that "all have sinned and fall short of the glory of God" (Romans 3:23). We all play a role in perpetuating or allowing racial bias to affect our lives—by acts of commission (conscious actions taken to perpetuate racism) or omission (things we don't do but could, to alleviate the problem).

The first step in addressing a problem is accepting the possibility that you may have one.

360 Degrees of Sight

A friend of mine became a professional counselor around the time I went into ministry about thirty years ago. Around that time she asked me, "Do you have any idea how people perceive you?"

Immediately I blurted out, "I'm from New York, so I don't really care!"

I was joking—sort of. I realize having that attitude isn't a good thing. There are truths people know about us that we don't know about ourselves. And we *need* to care about them, because those blind spots are preventing us from being the best people we can be.

In large organizations, it's common to conduct what's called a "360-degree evaluation." The process involves asking peers, those you report to, and those who report to you, about what they perceive to be your strengths and weaknesses:

> *In your opinion, what's holding Jim back? If you could tell him one thing that would help him be better at work, what would it be?*

This exercise reveals blind spots in very powerful and sometimes painful ways. Yes, the truth can hurt, but walking around with blind spots, especially when it comes to how we treat each other, causes pain for a lifetime—even for generations.

Next Steps

1. Can you name a time you have been hurt by someone else's blind spot? Which one?

2. Can you give an example of how one of the nine blind spots applies to your life?

3. Can you come up with a blind spot that I did not include?

Prayer

The way of a fool is right in his own eyes,
But he who heeds counsel is wise.
A fool's wrath is known at once,
But a prudent man covers shame. (Proverbs 12:15–16)

Lord, please open the eyes of my heart and nurture a humble attitude, one that can receive the truth about myself. Show me how blindly I have been in hurting others and, more important, how I can honor others. Holy Spirit, give me a forgiving heart toward those who have hurt me unknowingly. Grant me the wisdom and patience to reveal their blind spot to them in a way that I would want to be enlightened.

In Your powerful name I pray. Amen.

CHAPTER 7

The Third Option, Revisited

"#@% the Rock Church!"*

The words were like a knife in my heart. People were cursing left and right, but this time it was personal. I immediately jerked my head up to see who called out the church I pastor.

Then, a moment later, the same voice shouted, "#*@% Pastor Miles!"

Now I was really mad. My eyes raced back and forth, trying to see who had called me out. All I could see were shadows and cell phones filming the scene. But I'd soon be face-to-face with that voice—and have a very unexpected conversation.

Protesters were jammed together in a tight semicircle that pulsed with anger just two feet in front of me. They were outraged and frustrated because another Black man had been killed by a police officer, this time in laid-back San Diego. Ugandan immigrant Alfred Olango was killed on September 27, 2016, and this crowd had showed up at the El Cajon Police Department, just outside of San Diego, to demand answers. The city erupted in protests as news of Olango's death went viral, so I wasn't surprised when hundreds gathered at the police station.

A press conference was called the day after the tragic incident occurred, and I was part of the pastoral team that had been assembled to help provide a pastoral perspective. Since I'm a pastor and leader in the community, with close, personal ties to the police department, my job wasn't to take sides but to pray for peace, clarity, and reconciliation in the community.

After the press conference concluded inside the station, the police chief, three fellow community leaders, and I felt it was best for the chief to address the protesters outside. The plan was simply for the police to be as transparent as possible. I was just a person standing in the background, playing a behind-the-scenes role in helping both sides maintain open lines of communication.

So I was surprised and upset when someone directed their hostility toward the church and me.

Over the years, I've identified two common elements in the national dialogue on communities of color and law enforcement. First, there's always a passionate and heated interchange that pits the community against law enforcement, making relations between the two even more strained. Second, culture always challenges those standing on the sidelines to choose a side. *Who are you for? Who are you against?*

In the wake of Alfred Olango's death, I knew these were questions I would need to address as a pastor, which led me to pray for God's wisdom in determining what His Third Option would be.

The Mourning After

The morning after the press conference, I had a meeting with thirty pastors from our staff who represent Black, White, Latino, and Asian ethnicities—every perspective you can imagine. We often engage in conversation about what's going on in the community, but this meeting assumed a totally different tone than normal. It felt like everyone was taking a side—and for good reason.

One of our White pastor's family members, a law enforcement officer, had to go to work in riot gear that whole week to face the protesters. This increased the level of danger for him and his family.

An African American pastor was frustrated because, from his perspective, this was just another case of abuse of power. He described his need to tell his son how to carefully respond to the police if he was ever stopped. He felt this kind of warning to show deference was the only way to make sure his son didn't face a similar fate as Alfred Olango.

One of our White pastors had a one-year-old girl, and he confided that he couldn't imagine needing to tell his daughter about how to respond to the police. He said this with sad recognition of the reality that people of color live with.

Another White pastor, and former police officer, expressed the burden police carry when they do have to shoot and kill someone. He felt sympathy for what he assumed the police officer and his family were going through, not only because he'd taken a man's life, but because his actions were now being scrutinized and argued about publicly.

A Latino pastor shared how he had once been asked about his gang affiliation during a traffic stop. This was while his White wife and four kids sat with him in their minivan.

As I listened to these perspectives, the tension in the room was building and my mind was racing. *If these pastors are so divided, how much more divided will the twenty thousand diverse congregants of my church be this Sunday?* I wondered.

Sunday was coming, and I needed to prepare my message. I knew I needed to speak to this situation. What side would I be on? What position would I take? There were two distinct sides forming in response to this issue.

On one side, if you showed support for the police department, you were characterized as being against the Black community. Some equated this with being a racist.

On the other side, if you expressed support for the person who was shot, you were seen as hating on the police.

There seemed to be no middle ground.

"Skittles" Church

As I've mentioned, our church, the Rock Church, is one of the most diverse churches in the country. The ethnic diversity in our congregation matches that of our diverse city, so I knew that on Sunday I would literally be speaking to every conceivable perspective. The Rock Church represents every socioeconomic class, race, and ethnicity in San Diego. Homeless people, gang members, strippers, poor, wealthy, and everything in between sit next to each other every weekend during our services.

This diversity is true for all five of our locations, the local juvenile and state prison where our services are broadcast, and in all twenty services held throughout San Diego County each weekend—including the campus in El Cajon, located just a stone's throw from where the shooting occurred.

Our church is very well-known for the over $5 million of community service we provide throughout the county each year, including our support of the police department. We've done several "line-of-duty death" funerals—for the police, fire department, and the military—and we regularly partner with local government to serve San Diego.

So what was I going to say to our church family? What was I going to represent as God's response? Was there a Third Option in this tragic scenario?

On one hand, I could just mention the incident and pray, but that wasn't our "flavor." (*Flavor* means the way we normally do things.) I'd been on the news practically every day that week addressing the shooting and the daily protests. However, the last thing I wanted to do was appear to use the Bible to position one side against the other.

Thousands of African Americans, Latinos, and people of color who've had bad experiences with the police would be listening and watching. And sitting right next to them would be thousands of people who had no such experience with the police. I knew both sides were waiting to hear what I was going to say. So was I, and as of Wednesday of that week I had no idea what that would be.

Five Chairs

That Friday, I informed the Sunday production team to prepare a table and three chairs for the upcoming service. A sermon concept was forming in my mind, but it wasn't entirely clear yet.

Saturday night, as I was getting into bed, it hit me: I needed not three but five chairs. Sunday morning the stage was set with a table and five chairs.

One chair was labeled "Police." As I stood behind this chair during the service, I explained that, in my opinion, most police are trying to do the right thing. They are human beings with families, and with hopes and dreams. And in general I believe that about 1 percent of bad cops were ruining the reputation of the 99 percent of good cops. Whatever the actual percentages are, one bad cop is one too many, but most are good.

Then I stood by behind another chair labeled "Justified." This chair represented all the people who felt the recent shooting was legally justified, and the police officer did what he was trained to do under those circumstances. There were thousands of people in our church willing to sit in this chair.

I moved behind the next chair labeled "Unjustified." This chair represented people who believed the police officer acted prematurely in shooting the man. And right in front of me were thousands of people ready to sit in this chair.

Then I stood behind a chair with a red cloth on it. This chair represented the Liar, the Instigator, or the Accuser—a spirit of division challenging everyone to choose a side. The Liar stirs up negative rhetoric about those who don't believe what you believe, and those who don't hold all your views. He tells you that you must never agree or talk with them. He surrounds you with people who agree with you and reinforce the same position.

What's ironic about the Liar is that he's speaking to both sides of the argument, turning one side against the other. Even though the police shooting of a Ugandan immigrant was the incident in question, it opened all the old arguments—and old wounds—of a bigger racial issue.

Finally, I stood behind the fifth chair. This chair held the key to my message. This was the chair of unity. This chair was the heart of God. This chair represented the response I was going to propose. But before I could offer the solution, I needed to ask a few more questions of the congregation.

What is your heart toward people who don't agree with you?

Are you willing to honor their right to be heard?

Are you willing to acknowledge their pain and learn about their perspective?

Honor Power

There's no question that many people have had bad experiences with the police and therefore have reasons to mistrust them. And there are those who've had good experiences with the police and have good reason to trust them. There was a video of the shooting, which in theory would clear up any question about the matter. But in fact the video only reinforced everyone's position that their own version of the story was true.

In reality, all of our experiences are just that: *our* experiences. As real and legitimate as they are to us, there's always another perspective and a different solution to consider. But how can we represent our experiences and perspectives while learning from each other's, and work together to come up with a solution we can all stand behind?

For that, we need the Third Option: unity through mutual honor.

When we've been led to believe that we must choose one of two sides, we must *always* recognize it as a *false* dichotomy—a snare set by the Liar himself.

Reconciliation

We all want our experiences to be validated and our voices heard. We all want a legitimate opportunity to work toward solutions to real problems. We all struggle to honor the experiences and viewpoints of others. But there's only one way to honor ourselves and others in the process: by choosing the Third Option.

At the end of the sermon that day, we called people to the front of the church for prayer. As usual, several dozen people of all races and nationalities came forward, and I shook each person's hand, as I always do. A tall, African American, twentysomething young man grabbed my hand, held on, and pulled me close to him.

"I'm the guy who yelled at you the other night," he whispered.

"Whaaaaaat? Man, you gotta be kidding me," I answered.

My mind went back to that moment at the police station, and all kinds of emotions raced through my heart and mind, including how frustrated I'd been. Now, just a few days later, I was overwhelmed with relief that something in the message had spoken to him. I was also blessed that he came to church in the first place.

I met with him after the service, asking why he had said what he said, and asked what had moved him to get up out of his seat and walk to the front today. He replied, "I said those words out of anger and hurt. I said them out of disappointment and frustration, because I didn't feel you were saying anything about all the shootings."

His mother, who was also in the room, just about jumped out of her seat and slapped him upside his head. She said, "How can you say that he hasn't been talking about the shootings? He put pictures on the video screens of the people who were killed and brought people on-stage for prayer!" She was referring to how I'd responded to other similar shootings in the months prior to this one. Unfortunately, this brother hadn't been in church on those days. Go figure!

Then I asked him why he had come forward that day. He admitted he realized he'd been disrespectful and that I understood where he was coming from as a young Black man. For both of us, it was honoring to be heard and to feel understood. His humility opened the door to reconciliation and unity.

His apology gives me hope that change is possible. The young man's negative outburst toward me that night at the police station was not a race-based comment: we're both Black! Rather, it stemmed from a need for his value, pain, and experience as a Black man to be acknowledged. He perceived me as someone who didn't care—a member of his "emotional" out-group—someone who didn't understand his pain. His misperception was the reason he had reacted the way he had at the police station. He assumed I had chosen sides and that I was on the "other" side. He didn't see the Third Option.

He also assumed that I didn't know and couldn't relate to what he was going through—only to find out that he was just misinformed.

Understanding and Honor

You may be thinking, *How can I ever really know what someone is going through?*

When it comes to matters of race, you may never completely under-stand what someone who looks different from you feels in their heart. But you can honor that person by validating their pain as real and learning more than you already think you know about their perspective. You can acknow-ledge that people of your out-groups hurt just like those of your in-group.

Even though we look at a situation and label it as being about race, it's really more of a matter of respect and honor—or lack thereof. When people don't honor each other's perspective or experience—or give them an opportunity to be heard and validated—it hurts.

I thanked the young man for coming forward, which was a huge step to-ward healing his heart and mine. We experienced mutual honor and respect. This didn't mean the larger societal problem was fixed, but before society can be healed, the individual conflict within our hearts must be healed.

Which Side Are You On?

Let's revisit the story I told in the book's introduction, and dive a little deeper into Joshua's decision to pursue the Third Option.

Joshua was leading the Israelites into the Promised Land, around the year 1400 BC, and he knew he would face many opposing armies. As he was entering this new territory, he was confronted by a particu-larly impressive-looking soldier with his sword drawn and ready. Joshua asked the soldier, "Are you on our side or our enemies' side?" The sol-dier gave a startling response.

> *"Neither," he replied, "but as commander of the army of the Lord I have now come."* (Joshua 5:14)

Imagine asking someone whether they like chocolate or vanilla ice cream better, and having them answer *cheeseburger*. The Third Option sometimes seems bizarre to our limited understanding.

In effect, the messenger of God said, *No. I'm not on either side. I Am the side. I am holding not a sword of division, or an in-group–out-group sword, of "us" versus "them," but the sword of unity. I only support My plan, and My plan is unity. Honor My plan.*

Racial unity is not our idea; it's God's idea, and it's a much bigger issue than we can tackle on our own. We've seen what happens when people try: the division deepens and the situation worsens. The reality is, we need God's help. As a pastor, I see Him unifying people in our "Skittles" church—not in just a few dozen people, but in many thousands from all over San Diego County.

I can tell you the answer isn't in choosing the "right" side or the "right" people. The answer lies in humbling ourselves and serving a purpose that's bigger than any side or any one of us.

We can choose sides, or we can choose honor. But we can't choose both. What will you choose?

Next Steps

1. Describe the types of people whose opinion about things race related are opposite yours.

2. Describe what feelings you harbor in your heart toward them.

3. What would be one thing that would need to be communicated to bring your hearts one step closer? Be the one to say it!

Prayer

"And if it seems evil to you to serve the Lord, choose for yourselves this day whom you will serve, whether the gods which your fathers served that were on the other side of the River, or the gods of the Amorites, in whose land you dwell. But as for me and my house, we will serve the Lord." (Joshua 24:15)

Holy Spirit, forgive me for choosing sides in the past. Please help me learn from Joshua's example, and recognize that I can either choose to side with man, or choose to side with You. Strengthen my desire to always choose You, so that I can experience an honor shift in my heart toward those I would naturally choose to side against. Help me see things from Your perspective, and to obey You by always choosing the Third Option.

In Your name I pray. Amen.

CHAPTER 8

The Golden Rule

Have you listened to your heart lately?

A White girl named Dorothy grew up in the predominantly Black culture of Jamaica in the West Indies. Her parents, concerned that she would date and eventually marry a Black Jamaican man, moved her to Jamaica, Queens, New York, when Dorothy was a young teen.

One day Dorothy called her parents with some important news. "Uh, see, Mom and Dad, what had happened was . . . I met this guy."

That's right. She met, and eventually married, a Black, West Indian, Jamaican from—you got it—Jamaica, Queens. This was in 1934, where such a thing was illegal in most states. They married and had four children—three sons and one daughter named Margaret. She grew up and also married a Black man from Jamaica, and also lived in Queens, New York.

Dorothy lived less than a mile away from her daughter and her family. Since her husband passed away at an early age, she went everywhere with her daughter's family: camping, football games, baseball games, you name it. Just about every holiday was celebrated at Dorothy's house, enjoying her famous dish of rice and peas.

Sacrificial Love

Dorothy grew to be an older White lady with a soft-spoken Jamaican accent, constantly surrounded by dozens of loud Brown people.

But her grandkids never knew anything about *her* parents and siblings. Every now and then they would wonder, *Where did Grandma come from? And why won't she talk about her upbringing?* She had her secret, and it was the elephant in the room.

Many years later they learned that when she decided to marry her Black Jamaican husband, her parents and siblings cut her off completely. When her grandkids finally learned the full details of her story, they were old enough to understand the sacrifice her love had driven her to make.

You see, Grandma Dorothy is my grandma, and her daughter, Margaret, is my mom. Because of love, she endured the pain of rejection from her biological family. Because of love, she embraced a brand-new life with people who didn't look like her.

When we hear about the Golden Rule—treating others like we want to be treated—we often think of a feel-good kind of love. But love is only golden when it's worth sacrificing for. To love someone is to want what God wants for them and to be willing to be a conduit for them to receive it, even if it costs you dearly.

Nothing is more valuable than the ability to sacrifice for others. It's this kind of love that conquers all forms of hate and dishonor. Only this kind of self-sacrificial love can empower us enough to honor those who look different. Anything less than self-sacrifice dishonors our ability to love in the way God empowered us to.

Before you can honor someone from your out-group, it's important to know the true nature of the love we've been designed to express. As good as your intentions may be, it's possible that the version of love you express actually dishonors others, rather than honors them.

God Knows My Heart, but Do I?

As a staff meeting of a local church was about to end, the manager looked up and announced with a smirk, "Our next meeting will be Monday at 10:00 a.m. That's 9:30 for you Mexicans." When he saw the look of shock on the employees' faces, he quickly added, "Oh, you know what I mean. God knows my heart. I did not mean anything by it."

Have you listened to your heart lately? God does know your heart, and, thankfully, He loves us enough to patiently transform it.

> *The heart is deceitful above all things,*
> *And desperately wicked;*
> *Who can know it?* (Jeremiah 17:9)

It's so important to know your own heart, and one of the best ways to do that is to listen to how you talk to, and about, yourself. Chances are, your heart has issues with you, and you might even have some funky version of love for yourself. You can't truly love people more than you love yourself.

Jesus said, "'You shall love the Lord your God with all your heart, with all your soul, with all your mind, and with all your strength.' This is the first commandment. And the second, like it, is this: 'You shall love your neighbor *as yourself.*' There is no other commandment greater than these" (Mark 12:30–31, emphasis added).

How critical are you of yourself? That's at least how critical you are of others. Do you doubt yourself? You'll almost certainly doubt the ability and potential of others. How much do you believe in yourself? That's how well you're going to believe in someone else. How do you talk to and about yourself? Your words are not only a revealer of how much you love, or hate, yourself; they also reveal the highest level of love you'll be able to express to someone else.

If you try to love people without loving yourself, you'll fail. If you try to honor others without showing honor to yourself, you'll never get it right. God loves you, which gives you inherent value. It's an insult not to love yourself as He loves you, because you're telling God that He has a wrong view of who you are.

We need to tune in to the right view of ourselves, and tune out wrong views. And when we do, we can get a right view of others as well.

Racism Renames Yous

As a child, every classic Western movie I watched depicted Native Americans as savages. The producers made it very clear who the good guys and bad guys were. I remember wanting to know more about how the Native Americans lived. But the only frame of reference I had were images of scalpings and sounds of broken English. Black people have similarly suffered from such "mislabeling" throughout our nation's history.

Stereotyping people with derogatory terms—such as the N-word, *those people, boaters, poor white trash,* etc.—stigmatizes them as being less than worthy of love. Worse, some people call *themselves* by these names, internalizing the insults hurled at their families over generations and at themselves over their lifetimes. If a person does that long enough, he or she will begin living down to the meaning of the names others have given them. Not only do these terms dishonor the divine image we all possess, they give us an excuse not to love others. Sub-human labels give us an "out" for self-sacrificial love, fuel implicit bias, and become ingrained in us.

We all know the Golden Rule is to love your "neighbor" as yourself, but what if I label a person as something other than my neighbor? Do I still need to love them?

If someone says, "I love God," and hates his brother, he is a liar; for he who does not love his brother whom he has seen, how can he love God whom he has not seen? (1 John 4:20)

What if they are not my "brother" or "sister"? Do I still need to love them self-sacrificially?

When we label someone, consciously or unconsciously, as something other than our neighbor, our brother, or our sister, it disqualifies them from being someone we need to love. It gives us a pass, in our own selfish minds, to treat people any way we feel they should be treated. Their entire group can actually become "disposable" to us personally and in the broader context of society.

Instead of loving, we disrespect, demean, and mistreat. Instead of seeing others as valuable and lovable as we are, we categorize them as "optional" or "dispensable."

When we see another person as "less than," mistreatment seems appropriate and acceptable.

When we fail to dignify other humans with the label their God image deserves, we dishonor and minimize the eternal value that God has given them.

What's worse, we dishonor ourselves because we're behaving in a subhuman manner. We lower the standard of love we were created to give.

Love Hopes for All Things

A few years ago I was standing in a doorway, facing Donovan State's prison yard, preparing to take the stage to speak. The five hundred men in front of me were all dressed alike, in bright orange jumpsuits. Despite their uniform clothing and circumstances, they had self-segregated by skin color.

As I looked at the mosaic of faces, an overwhelmingly peaceful presence came over me, and my heart heard these words: *Tell those guys that I love them.*

I responded back to God, *Of course I'm gonna tell them that You love them: I always say that somewhere in my sermons.*

I then heard: *Look at them. I created these guys to be leaders, warriors, dads, uncles, coaches, and teachers. But they are living like animals in cages. They are locked away from their wives, children, and dreams. Tell them I'm not mad at them; tell them I love them.*

That day, God broke my heart for what broke His. My eyes welled up with tears of compassion for every single person on the yard. I knew it was God speaking to me.

Those men needed to be convinced that God really did love them even though they were in prison for what they'd done. Yes, even though they had murdered, raped, and robbed, they needed to know that what they heard weren't just the words of a preacher but the true heart of God speaking to them.

Are you willing to allow Him to express His love through you to whomever, whenever, and wherever? We dishonor God, ourselves, and our neighbors when we decide how, when, and with whom to share His love.

The men in prison needed to receive the hope and encouragement that the love of God brings. But in order for this message to be given with God's power, I had to love them first. And there was no way I could love them unless I knew that God loved *me* first. As I prayed for the right words to say, God filled my heart with His love, which overflowed into love for them. When I finally spoke, my words were His. But without the love of God in me, I simply *could not* have loved those guys in a way that pleased and honored Him.

And neither can you.

Racial reconciliation won't happen until we can love each other with a Godly love that takes over our will and breaks our hearts. But first we must understand what love is and what love is not.

Contract or Covenant

I've counseled hundreds of married couples over the years, and I've noticed a pattern. I've come to see that most marriages that end in divorce do so because of a flawed concept of honor and love.

When spouses are asked to rate how they *give* in the relationship, compared to how much they *receive*, they always overestimate the good they give and underestimate the good they receive. My guess is that this is true not only of marriages but of all relationships.

Consequently, instead of reflecting unconditional love as we were intended to do, we express a flawed version of love. We end up with a social agreement—a contract versus a covenant—that sounds like this:

> *I'll be nice if you are nice.*
>
> *I'll be patient to the degree that you are patient.*
>
> *I'll love you to the degree that I believe you deserve to be loved.*

We compare each other to our own sense of goodness, our individual standard of right and wrong. But a *covenant* of love doesn't operate like that. A covenant offers love no matter what the other person does, because they are worthy by design. The image of God in you and everyone you meet is always worthy of love. Therefore, the ability to express the loving heart of God is always possible.

Because my wife and I have been happily married since 1984, I am often asked our secret to a healthy relationship. I tell everyone who asks that our secret is *serving one another unconditionally.* Trust me, we don't do this perfectly. My wife has a long way to go! Seriously, though, we (mostly I) have to work constantly at this together because we're aware and intentional about our common goal.

Our culture has turned the concept of love into an emotional expression of kindness that's optional, depending on how we feel at the moment. It's a selfish definition of love that is focused on *me*. Because of this, love has become something we *selectively* distribute to those we like, when it's convenient and self-serving.

Jesus said, "You have heard that it was said, 'Love your neighbor and hate your enemy.' But I tell you: Love your enemies and pray for those who persecute you, that you may be sons of your Father in heaven. He causes his sun to rise on the evil and the good, and sends rain on the righteous and the unrighteous. If you love those who love you, what reward will you get? Are not even the tax collectors doing that? And if you greet only your brothers, what are you doing more than others? Do not even pagans do that? Be perfect, therefore, as your heavenly Father is conform" (Matthew 5:43).

His love is unconditional, never changing, and undeserved. Instead of waiting for us to transform our lives so that we become lovable, His love transforms our lives. If we're going to truly honor those who seem so different than we do, we must have a clear understanding of, and commitment to, the version of love that's true to His original design. When God inspired me to tell the inmates that He loved them, the only option I had was to do what God said, in the way He would have done it, to honor His purpose. After all, to love God is to obey God (1 John 5:3).

Love is a covenant to represent the heart of God, whether I feel like it or not, and whether I understand it or not. There are no contractual loopholes—no ifs, ands, or buts—when it comes to love.

Love Tells the Truth

Love is anchored in truth. Therefore, it doesn't always look like a romantic comedy or read like a Hallmark card. In fact, love requires us to speak the truth with respect and honor—even when doing so may hurt someone's feelings and potentially jeopardize a relationship.

Stephen A. Smith, of ESPN's *First Take* program, embodies this kind of love, and has a masterful way of calling a player out while at the same time showing love and respect.

In one particular incident, he responded to a player accusing his "haters" of being racists—of not liking him simply because he was Black. The broadcaster was determined to set the record straight. Here's my paraphrased Stephen A. Smith imitation, with the name of the player removed:

> *I got nothing against you, brother. I got your back. I've had you on the show, but I must say without equivocation, hesitation, or any indication of doubt in my thought process, sometimes people just don't like you simply because of you.*
>
> *White people, Black people, Latino people, Asian people, and everyone who checks the "other" box on the Census can dislike you, and it has nothing to do with race.*

Does this sound like love to you? It does to me.

Faithful are the wounds of a friend,
But the kisses of an enemy are deceitful. (Proverbs 27:6)

Would you rather have someone confront you when you need it, or lie about how awesome you are? What about when someone confronts or criticizes someone of a different ethnicity? When someone confronts you, it doesn't always mean it's about race. If someone doesn't like you, it might simply mean you did something wrong. The honorable thing to do is consider if there's something to learn from the criticism. Honor your ability to receive criticism and grow from it.

If a dude—someone from your out-group—says you have a big head, don't turn it into a racial thing. Look in the mirror and check your skull. You may actually have a big head. *Stop trippin'!*

Love is not a feeling or emotion. Love is about obedience to God, even when it's uncomfortable.

Do you love yourself enough to break out of your current comfortable mind-set? Do you love yourself enough to be obedient to God's command and make your life an example of honor in action?

If you do, begin right now to embrace love as a choice, and put the Golden Rule into action by self-sacrificially honoring people, *especially* when you don't believe they've earned it. Grace, after all, is undeserved.

Next Steps

1. What derogatory name have you used to replace *brother* or *sister*, categorizing them as "less than"?

2. Finish this sentence: I express contractual (conditional) love when I withhold it from _____
   because they _____.

3. I will express covenant (unconditional) love to my new "brother"/"sister" this week by _____.

Prayer

If someone says, "I love God," and hates his brother, he is a liar; for he who does not love his brother whom he has seen, how can he love God whom he has not seen? (1 John 4:20)

Dear Lord, please give me a desire to love those who look different than me. I know that You are love and I have no right to create my own version of a God who only expresses love to those I feel comfortable with. Please fill my heart with Your loving presence and remove any obstacles my pride has erected, so that I may truly see others with Your loving eyes. In Jesus' powerful name I pray, Amen.

CHAPTER 9

I'm Sorry

"My only goal . . . was to hurt him."

Officer Andrew Collins, of the Benton Harbor, Michigan, police force, started his route by saying to himself, *I'm going to make sure I have another drug arrest today.*

Unfortunately, a Black man named Jameel McGee happened to be walking down the street as Collins passed by. The officer arrested him for drug dealing. McGee loudly proclaimed his innocence but was eventually sent to prison for the alleged crime.

After four years, Officer Collins, who is White, admitted to completely fabricating the report. Four years. Can you imagine serving four years in prison for a crime you didn't commit?

"I lost everything," McGee told a reporter. "[So] my only goal [when I got out] was to seek him . . . and to hurt him."

I Don't Deserve That

Officer Collins served eighteen months for theft, planting evidence, and fabricating reports. Jameel McGee served four years for a crime he didn't commit. After their release, both men stayed in Benton Harbor.

In 2015, both men found themselves working at the same Christian café run by Pastor Brian Bennett of Overflow Church.

"Honestly, I have no explanation. All I can do is say 'I'm sorry, please forgive me,'" Collins pleaded when he encountered McGee at church.

"That was pretty much all I needed to hear," McGee told the media. Apology accepted.

Once grace was extended, all was forgiven. The men eventually became friends, and have spoken together publicly about the power of forgiveness.

Jameel McGee explained that he didn't forgive only to help himself, or even for the sake of Andrew Collins, but "for *our* sake. Not just us, but for *our* sake." By *our sake* he meant that he forgave for the sake of the broader community.

Countless offenses and counteroffenses have broadened the racial divide in our communities. In order to stop the cycle and move toward healing and unity, someone has to say *I'm sorry*. And when they do, the response consistent with the image of God is, *I forgive you*. Both the apology and forgiveness are consistent with loving our neighbor and honoring the image of God in ourselves and in others. Refusing to apologize, and refusing to accept an apology, are dishonoring to the heart of God—a God who models unconditional forgiveness toward us.

> Bear with each other and forgive one another if any of you has a grievance against someone. Forgive as the Lord forgave you. (Colossians 3:13)

The "bandwagon effect" is the tendency for people to believe and do things because other people believe and do those things. Just as we follow the lead of those who dishonor and stereotype people, we can follow the lead of those who apologize and forgive. Someone needs to set an example. Why not us? Or, more specifically, why not you?

By taking a step toward apologizing or forgiving someone, you could singlehandedly establish a new bandwagon effect rooted in love and honor. Imagine how much healing and unity could occur as a result of your one step of obedience in this regard!

As you read this chapter, you may recognize the need to apologize and forgive a specific someone for something they've done. Or perhaps you need to release the burden of unforgiveness you've been carrying for years—an anger aimed at no one in particular, other than the general unfairness of our broken world. If you find yourself in either of these camps, I urge you to move forward in faith, and act in obedience to the call to forgive. Forgiveness will benefit not only you but everyone in your life and your community at large.

Even though Andrew had nothing to say but a heartfelt apology, he was holding on to the faith that his apology would be accepted. That was a huge step of faith, and it was one that ultimately paid off.

I have to believe that Jameel knew people were watching and that his humility would encourage others to let go of their anger, bitterness, and pain as well. His incredible show of forgiveness led to an honoring relationship with a man whom he had every right to be angry with for the rest of his life. When Jameel chose a higher calling instead—the call to love his enemy—he most certainly caused countless others to treat their "enemies" with the same God-honoring gesture. Again, one individual's decision to obey God initiated a ripple effect that had far-reaching consequences in Benton Harbor, Michigan—and so can yours, wherever you live.[22]

Define *Forgiveness*

Many people confuse forgiveness with approval of an offensive or harmful act. Others have the false idea that forgiveness erases accountability. Neither of these concepts captures the real nature of forgiveness.

Forgiveness means that you no longer hold someone responsible for healing the pain of an offense toward you.

Forgiveness is the desire to look past an offense and see a person acting in a way that's inconsistent with the character potential God has placed in them.

Forgiveness is embracing the reality that someone may have done something to you out of fear and not out of the courage they're capable of expressing.

Forgiveness recognizes that they may have acted out of ignorance or hatred, rather than the understanding or love they were designed by God to express.

In other words, forgiveness looks past what a person did and focuses, instead, on who they were meant to be.

Forgiveness is an expression of the heart of God toward someone who hasn't earned it. It stems from an overflow of the realization that none of us deserves God's grace, mercy, or love.

Forgiveness is possible because we were created in the image of a God who forgives us. Moreover, it's *required* of all who claim Him as Lord, as a precondition to receiving God's forgiveness in our own lives.

> *"If you forgive others the wrongs they have done to you, your Father in heaven will also forgive you. But if you do not forgive others, then your Father will not forgive the wrongs you have done."* (Matthew 6:14–15)

Freedom of Forgiveness

My friend Loureen recently shared her powerful story of forgiveness with me. She told me that she had just started high school when 9/11 occurred. Like all other Americans, she was afraid and confused by the attack on our nation. Hate crimes against anyone who looked "Arab" or "Muslim" spiked to an all-time high as our nation mourned and retaliated. Suddenly, she was aware of her ethnic identity in a way she had never been before.

Loureen attended a small private Christian school—which had its pros and cons in our post–9/11 world. While it encouraged an expression of our faith, it also became a bubble for limited perspectives. And with classmates who'd had very little exposure to diversity, being an Arab American suddenly took on new significance for Loureen at school.

Here's Loureen's story in her own words:

I was one of only two Middle Easterners in my class, which had never seemed relevant until after 9/11. Suddenly, class discussions led to jokes about my background. "Hey, towel-head!" or "What's up, sand N*?" became commonly accepted greetings from classmates and even those I'd considered to be friends.

When the hunt for Osama bin Laden was on, classmates and teachers would reference me as though I had some sort of inside knowledge as to his whereabouts. When Saddam Hussein was captured, I was asked whether I was sad. I attempted to explain to anyone who'd listen that not every Arab/Muslim is an extremist and that, in fact, most Arabs in the United States are actually Christian. That point seemed lost on most— the notion of an Arab also being a Christian. Ignorance was equally rampant amongst students and teachers alike.

As a young girl trying to find my place in society, I did not know how to process it all. I did not want to hold their words and actions against them, because I wanted to believe their hearts were pure. I wanted to believe that they were just misinformed. I also just wanted to fit in. Joke after joke, however, wore me down, and imbued me with a sense of shame regarding my identity.

I also realized that I was a very different person at home versus at school. At home, I "turned on" my family's cultural expression, and at school I "turned on" my American expression, because my family's culture was embarrassing and shameful in that context. Maintaining this division furthered the internalized racism in my life.

It wasn't until I enrolled in a Spanish class, led by a Norwegian teacher who was married to a Peruvian man, that I realized how beautiful cultural diversity could be. My teacher was married to someone from a very different cultural background—and was proud of it. Her example led me to realize that God finds pleasure in our cultural differences and that, when we embrace them, we become the truest form of who He created us to be.

I also began to see those who discriminated against me as victims of misinformation. I felt bad for them but refused to let their ignorance enslave me. I decided to fully embrace who I was, at school, at home, and everywhere else I went.

Things shifted quickly for me. I went from hiding my ethnic expression at school to becoming the VP of the International Club, coordinating cultural events. I saw a real need for my fellow classmates to become acquainted with different cultures in a positive manner—not just through the lens of the media.

I became so enamored with multiculturalism that I went on to study intercultural communications at Pepperdine University. There, I founded the first ever Middle Eastern organization on campus, called Middle Eastern Peace and Awareness (MEPA). While we were met with backlash at first, it ultimately proved to be a fruitful effort at elevating awareness and promoting dialogue.

This tension also fueled my desire for social justice. I ended up earning an MA in international relations, which led me to develop the Global Human, a digital platform that celebrates positive cultural storytelling.

I remember seeing one of the individuals from high school several years later at a reunion event. He remarked that he was impressed with what I had achieved academically and asked me for some advice on his educational journey. I found it all very ironic. The young boy who had once insulted my intelligence and ridiculed my heritage was now asking me for advice. I'm glad I was in a place—spiritually and emotionally—where I could receive him graciously, forgive him, and offer my assistance.

As Loureen's story proves, words have a way of enslaving people by giving them an identity that is inferior to that which God has given us.

Unforgiveness can also lead to internalized racism. When you begin to hurt *yourself* because you buy into the negative criticism of others, it manifests itself in shame over who you are. Failing to honor the image of God in yourself keeps you from pursuing the dreams God has placed in you. When that happens, racism wins and the world loses out, because it prevents you from becoming all that God has created you to do and be.

When you're bombarded by messages regarding your lack of worth, you must reject them or you'll internalize their negativity. You must acknowledge and release yourself from the lies of Satan in your heart and mind. This may include forgiving yourself for imposing a burden of self-denial.

Forgiveness opens your eyes to the reality that freedom can come from the same person or types of people who attempted to put you in bondage.

Loureen says that today she reflects on the power of choosing to forgive them in those moments, because if she had not done so, her future would have turned out very differently. If she had denied her ethnicity, she would have also denied the plight of her fellow Jordanian Americans and missed out on her calling in life. She's now able to celebrate, without shame, the many layers of her God-given identity as a Jordanian American.

Loureen's story perfectly illustrates how, when we choose the Third Option, we honor ourselves. By honoring ourselves, we are empowered to forgive others, and carry their burdens as though they are our own.

Forgiveness as Fuel

Here's what my good friend Sergio, who pastors the largest Hispanic church in San Diego, had to say about forgiveness:

> The first time I remember ever hearing a racial slur, it was directed toward my hero and mentor—my father. Salvador De La Mora was a successful entrepreneur who owned a lucrative landscaping business as well as several real estate properties. But to a young man in his teenage years, growing up in the affluent community of Santa Barbara, California, my father's skin color spoke louder than any accolade or accomplishment he achieved.
>
> My father saw the rage in my naïve eyes as I listened to his clients speak harsh, derogatory statements in English about the man I adored. Words like ignorant, lazy, stupid, and wetback were words that I had never before heard describe any De La Mora, much less my father. Listening to him be degraded over and over again in a language he didn't even understand planted a seed of resentment in my heart for these men.
>
> As I grew older and watched more of these painful interactions occur, the seed of resentment grew to a desire for retaliation. When I ex-

pressed my hatred for these men, my father's poignant response ripped out the roots of anger faster than they had been sown.

"Sergio, they may not like our race, but they will respect our results. Work harder than your anger to achieve results that help them understand what they do not know."

Those words turned forgiveness into fuel for success. They changed my life and perspective on racism and prejudice. I saw the ignorance rather than maliciousness. And, for the first time, I could forgive.

Forgiveness for me was more than overlooking the hurtful nature of the insults. It became the fuel that turned what was meant for evil in my life into a motivation to excel.

Unimaginable Forgiveness

In 2015, the same year Jameel McGee and Andrew Collins reconciled, a twenty-one-year-old White supremacist walked into a prayer meeting at a historically black church in Charleston, South Carolina.

After listening to the group for a while, Dylan Roof pulled out a gun and killed nine people.

Families and friends of the victims must have understood the power of forgiveness. They publicly forgave the shooter less than a week after the massacre. I imagine they felt intense resentment and hurt. And I can't imagine how they faced the killer in the courtroom as he stood before them in chains. Instead of looking away in hatred, they confronted the hatred with love, honoring God and honoring their lost loved ones.

In January 2017, Roof was sentenced to death for his crime. Forgiveness doesn't mean the offender is off the hook but that the burden can begin to be lifted off *our* hearts. Forgiveness means you and I don't have to live in torment.

True forgiveness, the kind that cleanses the soul and heals the mind, can only happen with God's help. Forgiveness can't be earned or deserved—but must be received freely, so that we can become pass-through entities of God's grace and mercy.

If the families and friends of the shooting victims could forgive a murderer, then we, with God's help, can forgive those who've hurt us. Someone can call you an illegal, claim you're a terrorist, deny you a job, fire you unfairly, or call you White trash, but they probably haven't killed someone in your family. We can choose to forgive whatever's been done to us.

We'll experience hurt. We'll have actions taken toward us that are racially motivated, financially motivated, or bound up in pride. But it's less about what happens to us and more about how we choose to respond that matters in the end.

Jesus was persecuted and forgave. We must also forgive as we've been forgiven. God forgives us completely and gives us the opportunity to be completely reconciled.

We have a serious blind spot when we expect quick and complete forgiveness from God, but we're not willing to quickly and completely forgive others. Forgiveness demands that we let go of vengeance and allow God to bring justice in His way and in His timing.

Forgiveness must also extend beyond those who've committed a direct offense against us. Sometimes we need to forgive an entire family, community, or race to live in peace.

Words Wound

A few years ago I was at an event, listening to an acquaintance, who happens to be Black, give a presentation. To my surprise, during some humorous opening remarks, he pointed to me and made fun of me for being "almost Black."

He got a big laugh out of it. I can still hear the audience but, more important, I can feel the disappointment and hurt. This wasn't exactly the reception I had in mind. To be honest, it took some time for the sting to wear off.

During the next few weeks, whenever I saw this person, I never thought about honoring him. *Avoidance* is the word I would use. But I noticed something happening in my heart. My unforgiveness was turning into resentment, anger, and a critical attitude. This was heading somewhere, and it wasn't somewhere good.

I needed to admit to God that I had negative feelings and ask for His help. I couldn't rely on my friend to heal my pain, but I knew speaking with him about my hurt could play a huge role in the healing process. So I initiated a conversation. I chose to honor his ability to hear me and his desire not to offend. I also had to honor my ability and responsibility to forgive him and not continue to think the worst of him. As a matter of fact, the longer I refused to forgive, the worse his offense became. My imagination created a narrative that was worse than reality.

I didn't want to communicate in a way that intentionally hurt him back, but let me tell you, I needed God to help me with this one! Thankfully, He did, and it became crystal clear during our conversation that my friend was very disappointed in himself. He apologized and asked for forgiveness, which I freely gave him. Even though he didn't intentionally hurt me, he understood how his words had caused me pain. I also recognized how my unforgiveness had enslaved me with lies about his intent and who he really was. Forgiveness resulted in freedom for both of us.

Is there someone you need to talk with? Someone you need to forgive? Don't wait any longer. Time apart can only heal so much. Without a conversation, true reconciliation cannot happen. People can't learn from their mistakes if they are not told that they've made any. People cannot apologize if they don't know they have been offensive, and if they are not made aware of their mistake, they may do it again. If you have bitterness, anger, jealousy, or envy toward someone, you can't and won't be able to honor them.

By carrying resentment in your heart, you'll hurt yourself far worse than anyone else can ever hurt you. Without forgiveness, resentment will fester in your soul, causing more damage to you than anyone your resentment is directed toward, ultimately preventing you from honoring God's purpose for your life.

Time Isn't Enough

For most of his life, my grandpa had an issue with God that I wasn't aware of. At the age of eighty-one, as my grandpa lay in bed consumed with cancer, I had the privilege of speaking with him, and sharing a message of forgiveness.

"Grandpa, I want to talk to you about Jesus."

He turned his head away from me and said, "Go ahead!" After I spoke for a few minutes about God's forgiveness, he said, "What about the White priest who was mean to my people?" He was referring to the Black Jamaicans in Kingston, where he grew up.

That's when I realized that Grandpa still held on to bitterness toward several men in Jamaica. This unforgiveness, over half a century old, was preventing him from receiving the love of God, which he fully understood but could not accept.

I explained how it's not right to blame God for the actions of people, even people who theoretically represent God. Eventually he prayed with me to receive his own forgiveness from God, opening the door to God's healing love in the final days of his life.

Life isn't fair. And guess what? Forgiveness isn't fair. We can't always make things right in this world, because we are all flawed—and, as we've established, people who have been hurt hurt others. What we can do instead is give up on the notion of "fairness" and choose the

Third Option of honor by deciding to make things right in our own hearts. In other words, it's our job to do our part, and leave the outcomes to God. That is *true* faith: trusting that God's plans for our lives—peace, joy, and love—are far better than we deserve. And it's *that* type of faith that will lead us into honoring relationships with others.

Children of Unforgiveness

Between the time I was offended by my friend, and the time we reconciled, unforgiveness gave birth to a few ugly children: resentment, retaliation, anger, and hate.

These feelings lied to me, telling me that if I let them express themselves and linger, I'd feel better. For about ten minutes, that felt true. What they *didn't* tell me is that ultimately, they'd enslave me.

These warped offspring didn't tell me they opposed the character of God. They didn't tell me they wanted to destroy my ability to love and honor others. No, they were much craftier than that. They snuck into my heart by legitimizing the anger I felt, and justifying feelings of vengefulness. They encouraged me to look away from God and to take things into my own hands—to nurture the hatred and feel justified in doing so.

Oh, what sneaky liars they were!

What I learned the hard way is that inflicting wounds on someone else's life—and holding on to the hatred in my heart—could never satisfy me or make things right. In the end, the only way to satisfy my heart was to do what pleased God: obey Him. God never calls us to hurt someone else in order to avenge a wrong done to ourselves. In fact, healing comes from blessing others, even at the expense of our own comfort.

The first step we take in expressing our freedom from harboring anger and its ugly children is the most important. Here's how Sam, one of my son's friends, did it.

Sam was getting his books out of his locker when a Mexican classmate in his elementary school called him a "Red dot from India" and told him to go back to his country. Later that day, with tears in his eyes, he told his mother what had happened. She was furious, but gathered herself and asked her son what he was going to do.

She knew that this might have been the first racial slur he had ever experienced, but it certainly wouldn't be the last.

She also knew that these were the kinds of experiences that would play a role in shaping her son's social narrative: how he viewed himself and those around him.

She knew it was important that he respond in a manner that honored his God-given potential to rise above the insult. To do that, he would have to learn to forgive the kid who'd hurt him.

She used the opportunity to teach Sam that forgiveness did not mean he approved. Rather, it would keep him from being held hostage to the ignorance of others. She also taught him an important lesson: that when someone is mean to you, it says nothing about you and everything about them. So whatever Sam responded would say everything about him, too.

She prayed that he would learn to forgive from a position of strength and freedom, rather than from a place of inferiority. The anger of man, she reminded him, would not produce the righteousness of God.

The next day Sam told the kid that he was wrong to call him a "Red dot from India," because he was actually a "Green dot Indian." And he told the kid that he forgave him for not knowing the difference.

In actuality, Sam was neither, but what he did demonstrate was the freedom that forgiveness provides. His forgiveness gave him freedom from the bondage that name-calling attempts to impose, and communicated that he was completely comfortable with his identity.

As Sam's story so poignantly illustrates, when you choose to forgive, you restore your own dignity in a way that enables you to honor yourself and others.

The Forgiveness Shift

How do you know if you've truly forgiven someone?

Anytime I find myself in an antagonistic relationship with someone else, I eventually realize that I am only arguing my point of view . . . with myself. My mind runs through all kinds of self-justifying scenarios to prove I'm right, but all I'm really doing is increasing my stress and ruining my beauty sleep.

At some point I recognize the need to forgive, so I go through the motions. I do what I think constitutes forgiveness, but a few minutes later I'll wonder, *If I just forgave them, why am I still arguing with myself in my mind?*

Sound familiar? How many nights have you lain in bed arguing with "someone else"—really, your own conscience—about what's happened or how you should respond?

As you're arguing with yourself, those homely children of your unforgiveness develop scenarios and rehearse hypothetical responses. They position your heart to express itself in a way that honors resentment, retaliation, anger, and hate instead of forgiveness and grace.

The only way you'll really know if you've forgiven someone is when the children of unforgiveness have moved out of your mind. You'll know they're gone when your thoughts become reflexively respectful and honoring to yourself and to others.

It will take time, but if we consistently honor our divinely endowed ability to express the forgiveness we've received from God, we'll experience freedom from the bondage and the lies that unforgiveness spouts.

Giving and Receiving

Is there someone *you* want an apology from? That apology may never come. But if you have a forgiving heart, you'll be able to survive and thrive in the face of pain.

Do you need to apologize to someone for something you've said or done? Do you need to apologize to yourself for what you've allowed yourself to believe or how you've mistreated others out of your own pain?

While Jesus was hanging on the cross, He said, "Father forgive them—they don't know what they're doing."

Think about that for a moment. Jesus was wrongly accused and had been crucified. Yet He chose to forgive His perpetrators. His radically loving heart lies at the heart of what lies at the heart of Christianity. Jesus lived his entire life in an attitude of continual forgiveness, and calls His followers to do the same: "But if you do not forgive, neither will your Father in heaven forgive your trespasses" (Mark 11:26).

The real decision isn't who and when we forgive but whether we'll choose to be like Jesus by choosing to have a forgiving heart.

In reality, those who attempt to oppress and insult you simply reveal their own fear and weakness, expressing cowardice rather than courage. Your forgiveness reminds them of how they were intended to love and honor you and others.

Next Steps

1. Is there someone that you claim to have forgiven but still argue with in your head?

2. Do you need to apologize to someone? Try this: Say his or her

name. Describe the offense: what you felt you did or said that was dishonoring to them. Be real. Express the emotion. Describe the pain that you think it might have caused, recognizing that the damage you inflicted was probably worse than you're able to acknowledge or admit.

Do not give a reason for why you did what you did: Just say sorry. Repentance has no defense. Simply say that you were wrong and ask for their forgiveness.

3. Do you have someone to forgive? Try this: Say his or her name. Describe the offense: what he or she did that hurt you. Be real. Express the emotion. Describe the pain it caused. Admit that there may be more to what happened than you realize. Take some time to vent, cry, or scream. Admit your need to forgive and your need for God's help in doing so.

"I no longer hold _____ responsible [is something you might say] to heal the pain of what they did. I forgive him/her. I release the burden of this pain to You, God, and ask You to help me honor them in spite of what I've experienced."

Prayer

Lord, when you were being ridiculed, beaten, and murdered, you prayed, "Father, forgive them, for they do not know what they do" (Luke 23:34). With Your help, I pray for _____ , and I forgive them. I know that they are created in Your image and I choose to honor You, and them, by forgiving.

In Jesus' name, Amen.

If you've hurt someone, you might say this prayer:

Lord, I have hurt someone and need to ask them for forgiveness. Please reveal to me why I did what I did, so that I may learn from my mistakes. Holy Spirit, prepare their heart for my confession, and please guide them in helping me understand how I hurt them. Please use them to help me learn from my errors, and change my heart.

In Jesus' name, Amen.

CHAPTER 10

Fear Factor

Being "the other" is the story of my life....

During a discussion about the burden of being the "other," a friend asked, "Why can't you just get over it?" I realized that she needed to experience "other-hood," or being the "other," herself—to walk a mile in someone else's shoes.

However, there was an unexpected blind spot to deal with.

Consequently, I recently asked several White people to voluntarily place themselves in a situation where they were the only White person. To help document these "field trips" I sent my friends on, I developed a simple questionnaire. I used the term *field trip* to make it seem like a fun assignment, but they didn't all see it that way at first. The "field trip" idea is the result of a lady challenging me to "just get over it." It seemed like the best way to give her a sense of being the "other."

In fact, each of these people felt uneasy when I initially presented them with the idea. Some stiffened up, others unknowingly expressed stereotypes about certain communities, and still others gave excuses about why they couldn't participate. The funny thing is, I never mentioned *which* community they were supposed to immerse themselves in. They could have chosen a place where everyone else was Asian, Latino, Middle Eastern, or Black, but they all just assumed I wanted them to go to the scariest, most dangerous places in their city.

It's logical for a person to feel uncomfortable being alone in a high-crime neighborhood, but a blind spot caused "danger" to be the first association with being among a group of people of color. Why not consider going to a church, a school, a friend's home, a shopping center, or an office complex? Even though for one guy those places were also scary. The Third Option owns this blind spot by acknowledging it as a dishonoring thought process. It then disowns it by going on the originally intended field trip.

Here's what I asked them to do on their "field trips":

"Walk in My Shoes" Field Trip

Thank you for accepting the challenge of the "Walk in My Shoes" Field Trip. The purpose of this exercise is to place yourself in an environment where you're a minority.

Please document your experience by completing the form below.

When were you asked to accept this challenge?

....

....

What did you feel emotionally?

....

....

What were your initial thoughts about what would or could happen?

....

....

What feelings did those thoughts stir in you?

....

....

Had you ever been in a similar environment before?

....

....

Describe your emotions and thoughts while going to the location:

....

....

Describe the location you went to.

....

....

Describe your feelings and emotions upon arrival.

....

....

Describe your experience.

....

....

Were any comments made to, or about, you?

....

....

How were you treated? Be specific.

....

....

What did you learn about yourself, your perceptions, and the people/group you encountered?

....

....

Additional comments:

....

....

Jeremy's Field Trip

Below is the report from Jeremy, a thirty-year-old White guy from the Midwest who decided to get a haircut at a Black barbershop.

What did you feel emotionally?

Initially, I thought it would be exciting, but at the same time, I had to pause and think to myself how I would find a Black barbershop. So, to find one, I asked an African American guy I had recently developed a relationship with.

When I told him about the challenge and asked his thoughts on a place I could go, he laughed. But as he thought about it, he said it was really cool that I wanted to try something like this.

Initial thoughts about what would or could happen?

Well, when I decided I was going to go to a barbershop, I felt a little nervous. I needed to get my hair cut anyway. Honestly, I was hoping there would be only four or five people, and that I could get in and out before the quarters expired in the parking meter.

I wasn't fearful of being beaten up or mistreated, but I was apprehensive about being the only White guy in the room.

What feelings did those thoughts stir in you?

I think my biggest thought was *Will I fit in?* The obvious answer was, *Heck no. You're going to stand out like a sore thumb.*

Describe your emotions and thoughts while driving to the location.

As I got closer, my hope that it would be a quick "in-and-out" crept into my mind. I also took more notice of the shops that lined the street. Normally I just drove through, paying no mind to the buildings; this time I paid close attention.

Describe the location you went to.

I went to a barbershop in a strip mall, with multiple shops around it. Most of the shops seemed run-down.

Describe your feelings and emotions upon arrival.

As I walked toward the barbershop, I peered into the window. It was the busiest barbershop I've ever set foot in! I saw about fifteen people just sitting by the window and thought to myself, *I'm going to be here awhile. This might be a little more awkward than I hoped it would be.*

Then I noticed a sign above the entrance that read, "We welcome all." And that helped set the stage for my experience.

Describe your experience.

I asked the closest gentleman to the door if there was a sign-in. He said, "Nope, you will know when it's your turn." I thought that was strange, but found an open seat.

It was then I really soaked in the environment. I looked around to see some of the guys watching a movie. One guy my age made a comment about the movie being terrible. I agreed.

I sat flipping through emails on my phone and looking up at the TV from time to time. I was thinking to myself, *Don't show that you feel out of place; just look "normal."* Then I thought, *My face is probably saying to everyone else that I feel uncomfortable.*

Just then I was called up by the head barber to get my hair cut. His name was Nate. I was treated like one of the guys.

How were you treated? Be specific.

As I approached the chair, Nate reached out his hand to shake mine and introduce himself. He was a twenty-five-year-old guy who seemed to be much like me when I was that age. He was just making ends meet, and seemed to enjoy being a barber.

We found a lot in common with talk about sports, and agreed that dating women was extremely difficult. We shared a good laugh over that. He said he was going through some relationship issues, like most guys, and we talked about that for a little while. It was a good conversation.

About halfway through our conversation, a young woman came into the shop selling tickets to the local fair. Nate said he wanted a couple. He then turned to me and said, "Hey, man, you want any?" I was kind of surprised to be asked, but I said yes. I mention this because even then, it was as if I was one of the "regulars." I was treated no differently than anyone else in the shop.

When Nate started to cut the very top of my hair, he said, "Hey, man, you have a little bit of a weave up here."

I honestly had no idea what that meant, but assumed it was like a Black guy's hair. My great-great-great-grandfather was actually Black. I actually had my hair in a 'fro style in high school.

What did you learn about yourself, your perceptions, and the people/group you encountered?

Overall this was a great experience. I didn't necessarily think I would have a whole "life story" type of conversation with the guy cutting my hair, but it turned out that way. It was a great conversation and a great haircut—better than where I normally go.

I think there might have been an initial *What is this White guy doing here?* feeling, but that could have just been me.

——————————

Jeremy moved from avoidance and anxiety to honor, because he was willing to move beyond his comfort zone in search of potential new relationships with people who were different than him. By the way, Nate is his new regular barber.

False Expectations

Jeremy had an unexpectedly great experience on his field trip. But one of the men I assigned this task to simply never did it. He later admitted he was too afraid to follow through.

Fear is sometimes referred to as an acronym for *false evidence appearing real*. In the case of racism, fear represents an expectation of emotional or physical harm that keeps us from connecting with those who look different from us.

Not only is fear a driver of racism, fear is also an ugly by-product of it. When you anticipate that people are going to reject you, hurt you, be offensive toward you, or accuse you, fear will take over and prevent you from engaging them in a meaningful way.

Is fear playing a role in your interactions, or lack thereof, with people of different races? Let's explore how to address those fears together.

Fear Is Dishonor

If we let fear control us, we're dishonoring ourselves and our ability to honor others. But if we channel our fear into honor, we'll make progress, personally and with others. Here's another way to address FEAR:

F—*Face the **Facts***.

E—*Get **Educated About the "Other."***

A—*Be **Accountable to Affirm One Another.***

R—*Build **Relationships, Recognizing the Image of God in Everyone.***

As I mentioned, when I proposed this field trip, each of the six people experienced some form of fear or nervousness.

I wonder how many of you reading this are experiencing anxiety just thinking about being the only person of your ethnicity in the room, or even sitting in a group of cars at a stoplight. Maybe you've experienced anxiety from some of the content in this book. Do you find yourself avoiding conversations about race? Do you get uncomfortable when the subject of race or racism comes up?

If this describes your feelings, I understand. Being "the other" can be very uncomfortable.

Now imagine what it's like to feel like this every day—to feel as if your every word and action is being observed, possibly scrutinized. Have you considered how that sense of unease could prevent you from following through on God's call for your life to honor others?

Have you considered how your fear has prevented you from seeing life from a different perspective? Imagine dealing with the awkwardness of being "the other" on a daily basis, for the duration of your life. (People of color reading this are probably thinking, *Being "the other" is the story of my life—welcome to the club.*)

Let's Redefine FEAR

F—Face the Facts

Four of the six individuals I asked to participate in the field trip took me up on the offer. One declined and had no further comment. But another who declined said the following:

> I was asked recently to go to a location where I would be the only White person.
>
> Immediately I felt uncomfortable. My mind raced with thoughts

of where I could go that would be safe, and considered what White friends I could bring with me.

In the city I live, there are very distinct areas of ethnicity. I live as far south as you can within the city limits from any African American communities. I would be increasingly concerned for my safety if I ventured northward. And, mostly for that reason, I never venture into that area.

I began to picture what it would be like standing in a restaurant, maybe a sports arena, or possibly an African American church, where I was the only White person. I knew I would feel nervous and conspicuous, that many eyes would be looking at me. I would assume they would wonder: What is that guy doing here in our place? *I'm sure I would want to leave as soon as I could. At the same time, I also thought that doing this would stretch me beyond my comfort zone, that 99.9 percent of the fears I had would not come close to happening, and I might just find a new friend or two.*

Each of the people I invited to take this challenge expressed some form of fear or apprehension about what they anticipated happening. I asked each of them if they had ever, in their entire life, experienced the treatment they feared. Every one of them said no.

All but two commendably chose to face their fears, and, as a result, their comfort zones were expanded and their ability to honor others grew. They all had fears based on preconceived ideas rather than facts.

If you face your fears, I'm confident you can get comfortable with being the "other." Fear of being the "other" will prevent you from developing honoring conversations, honoring relationships, and the unity we all desire.

The more comfortable you become with being the "other," the more you will enjoy interactions with people who are different than you, and the more equipped you will be to love and honor them.

E—Get Educated About the "Other"

Learn what you don't know about the people you fear or think you are resented by.

As William H. Willimon writes in his book, *Fear of the Other: No Fear in Love,* "In competition with other emotions, even strong ones like lust, fear seems to best them all in intensity of engagement of our whole limbic (emotional) system."[23] When we feel threatened, we think less clearly, have difficulty receiving and interpreting new information, make far more mistakes in perception, and respond negatively to situations—focusing on the downside and taking fewer risks.

Willimon suggests these fear factors mean "our responses to external threats are more knee-jerk defensive and less thoughtful." Fear and anxiety force us "into emergency mode, totally focused upon ourselves and our survival."[24]

Taz was six foot three inches and 280 pounds when I met him. He is a two-strike felon and has been involved in various White supremacist gangs. Ninety percent of his body, including his face, is covered with tattoos, everything from names of people he knows to swastikas.

He claims that most of his hatred toward others stems from hatred of self. When he lived in LA, he hung around Black gangs. When he lived in Reno, he joined a Tongan gang. And while living in Maine, he started an all White gang.

He, too, was motivated by fear. The fear he and his fellow gang members felt was made evident on a flier they placed on cars: *Don't let the minority become the majority.*

In San Diego, Taz started his own skinhead gang, some of whose members listened to reggae music. The entire time that he lived in San Diego, he had a Mexican roommate. These contradictions started to stir up questions in his own mind about how senseless—and ridiculous—his hatred was.

Eventually, Taz was stabbed in a gang fight. While he was fighting for his life, a Black surgeon—who Taz was supposed to hate—saved his life.

This Black doctor, while pulling tubes out of Taz's swastika-covered chest, asked Taz about his life and his family. He cared for a guy who obviously carried hatred toward him. This expression of love and honor moved Taz to ask himself, *What do I have against this Black guy and, more broadly, all Black people?*

It was the doctor's courage that inspired Taz to educate himself out of racism and into honor. Today, Taz works for a Black man. He sometimes introduces me to his former White supremacist friends, often bringing them to church to learn who the Author and Perfecter of love and honor is.

When you get educated, you'll be amazed at how quickly fear dissipates in your heart.

A—Be Accountable to Affirm One Another

Be accountable to yourself in your thoughts, actions, words, and even your perceptions of others. Look around and ask yourself: *Do my actions match my claim to love everyone? Does my personal experience—not what I see online or hear from my friends—match my fears?* Be accountable to yourself in facing your fears, rather than letting yourself be paralyzed by them.

At age nineteen, Joyce received a phone call with the good news that she landed the job she had applied for.

The next day she floated into the restaurant and introduced herself to the manager. He looked at her with a blank stare and asked, "How can I help you?"

"I'm here for the receptionist job."

He said, "We already hired someone."

"Yes, I'm Joyce. The one you hired."

He repeated himself, and Joyce again told him, "That's right, you called me yesterday and told me I was hired."

"This isn't going to work out," he mumbled as he reached into his wallet, handed her a five-dollar bill, and said, "Go back to your hood."

As she told me this story, she said, "When the manager interviewed and hired me over the phone, he was very complimentary and I was thrilled he had such confidence in me. But when he rejected me, I realized I was good enough on paper but not in the flesh. The real me, the Black me, was not good enough, and there was nothing I could've done to measure up."

For the next two years Joyce worked in a diverse, low-income neighborhood to avoid being treated unfairly again. She feared the rejection and humiliation of working in a White environment. Later, Joyce was referred by a White coworker for a job at a motorcycle dealership. The problem was, the company was in a mostly White neighborhood. That might not seem like a cause for concern to you, but for Joyce it was nearly a deal breaker.

Nevertheless, she faced her fear, became accountable for her own future, and applied anyway.

When she arrived at the dealership, she was literally shaking from fear. The first thing Joyce did was ask the manager if he would have any issue with hiring a Black person for the position.

The owner laughed and, after the interview, hired her on the spot. Over the next ten years she went from an accounting assistant to becoming the financial controller. She only recently left that job to be a pastor at our church.

Most people get nervous about job interviews. But can you imagine being fearful simply because of the color of your skin? Have you ever asked a friend of a different race whether they've had a similar experience—the fear of an interview, or going to a place to eat, or walking into a church—because they were concerned about how they'd be judged for how they looked?

In order to honor the individuals we meet, we must separate the acts of certain individuals from the acts of a racial group as a whole. Instead of letting our past experiences frame a narrative and confirm our "suspicions," we must consciously fight through the fear of our next encounter, believing that there are wonderful people of all ethnicities who welcome and affirm our value.

R—*Build Relationships, Recognizing the Image of God in Everyone*
Chris Rock jokingly said, "All my black friends have a bunch of white friends. And all my white friends have *one* black friend."

In fact, data from the Public Religion Research Institute shows that 75 percent of Whites have "entirely white social networks without any minority presence." The same holds true for slightly less than two-thirds of Black Americans.[25]

Jeremy knew he could go to a Black barbershop because he recently developed a relationship with an African American guy, and through their casual conversations they developed trust. Their relationship started like any other, on common ground: talking about football, camping, and what they both did as kids.

Fear gets in the way of honorably engaging with people who don't look like us. Relationships, however, destroy fear.

Tom's Field Trip

I was initially anxious, and somewhat concerned, that I would be going into an unsafe area. I went to a coffee shop in a predominantly Black and Hispanic neighborhood. Most of the other customers had tattoos and many were overweight. I noticed one other White male during the time I was there.

I did feel like an outsider, but people were friendly. The prices were cheaper than the Starbucks I've been to, which was interesting. I sat at a table, ate a snack, and tried to engage in conversation. No one was interested in having a conversation, but I didn't feel threatened. After I finished, I walked around the strip mall and noticed people coming and going. Nearly everyone was dressed differently than me.

Most people were polite, and most people looked at me as if I was different. After taking a complete lap around the shopping center, I walked into a small grocery store hoping to engage in conversation.

I held the door open for several ladies who were entering the store. I said hello, and they smiled politely but walked away.

The food in the store was different than the food in the stores I shop in. I noticed a larger selection of Hispanic food and more junk food and soft drinks—very little fresh food. I grabbed a twenty-four-ounce bottle of name-brand water from the cooler near the checkout and got in line to pay. When the checker said the price was $1.05, I almost fell over. That same bottle of water in my neighborhood would be nearly three dollars.

My biggest takeaway was I learned what it felt like to be different than everyone around me. I didn't feel threatened or judged; I just felt different, which might be how a Black person feels when walking around some neighborhoods.

God created us all different. No one better or worse, just different. We need to celebrate the differences and enjoy each other. Sadly, we've allowed society to create a barrier. This barrier precluded me from engaging in conversations today, but I'm confident that same barrier exists for other people when they come into my neighborhood.

I'll be more intentional about engaging with people of all races in the future.

Fear Versus Unity

Fear is the enemy of unity. And unity is the only option worth fighting for.

Being uncomfortable isn't a legitimate excuse for avoiding those who don't look like you. We are all called to be part of the healing process in our country's racial divide. And it all starts with one small step out of our comfort zones, where life-transforming conversations take root and form a foundation for real relationships.

Fortunately, there's a way out of feeling like you have to live in a bunker—and it sounds like this: *I want to get to know you. I want to understand you, and I don't know how. I don't want to say the wrong thing, but I might. I give you permission to correct and redirect me. Let me in and be gentle with me as we figure this out together.*

This relational shift takes courage, and you'll feel vulnerable while you're doing it, but it's 1,000 percent worth it.

Next Steps

1. Take the "Walk in My Shoes" Field Trip.
2. Complete the form included earlier in the chapter and share what you learned with others.
3. Commit to joining another person on their first field trip.

Prayer

You did not receive the spirit of bondage again to fear, but you received the Spirit of adoption by whom we cry out, "Abba, Father." The Spirit Himself bears witness with our spirit that we are children of God, and if children, then heirs—heirs of God and joint heirs with Christ, if indeed we suffer with Him, that we may also be glorified together. (Romans 8:15–17)

Lord, I ask that You empower me to live a life based on truth, not fear. Fill my heart with Your courage so I can move past fear and begin to love others like You do. Please show me when I'm operating out of fear so I can choose courageous honor instead.

In Jesus' name, Amen.

CHAPTER 11

The Privilege of God

A different, more honorable form of privilege was emerging.

A group of ten executives, representing some of the nation's most successful companies, stood across from ten inmates in one of the nation's most dangerous prisons.

These executives had volunteered to spend the weekend mentoring inmates for a prison entrepreneurship program led by Defy Ventures. Defy is a nonprofit that capitalizes on inmates' expertise in running criminal organizations by teaching them how to "transform their hustles" into legitimate business enterprises. Defy is one of the most successful prison programs in the nation, thanks to a five-year track record of dropping recidivism rates from 76.6 percent to 3.2 percent among its graduates.

Standing ten feet apart from each other in two parallel rows, executives lined up shoulder to shoulder on one side, mirrored by the inmates standing across from them. The name of the game was "Step to the Line," and everyone in the room answered the same questions at the same time. Those who answered yes stepped forward. Those who didn't stayed in place.

If you had two parents who tucked you in at night and told you they loved you, step forward.
None of the inmates stepped forward, all but one of the executives did.

If you went to a school where you didn't fear gang violence, and where you had up-to-date books and technology, step forward.
Not one inmate moved, but all of the executives did.

If you had breakfast every day before school and took a packed lunch with you to school, never going through your day on an empty stomach, step forward.
Same result.

If you had more than fifty books in your home, step forward.
Same result.

If you grew up with an immediate family member in prison, step forward.
All of the inmates stepped forward; none of the executives did.

If you lost a family member due to gun violence while you were a child, step forward.
Same.

If you were addicted to drugs before the age of twenty, step forward.
All of the inmates stepped forward, and only two of the executives did.

Tears welled up in the eyes of everyone present: the inmates over memories of their broken childhoods; the executives because their hearts broke for the inmates. This striking representation of privilege— something most executives rarely recognize, much less acknowledge— highlighted the stark differences between those who'd been raised in nurturing environments and those who'd barely survived their youth. BTW, not all of the executives in the prison were white.

After this experience, one executive referred to his advantage or privilege as "winning the birth lottery," recognizing that the inmates, through no fault of their own, were born into less fortunate circumstances than his.

As awareness of the executives' privilege grew, however, *a different, more honorable form of privilege started emerging.* This new privilege these executives discovered was the privilege of *leveraging their experiences and advantages for the benefit of others.* I call this "the Privilege of God."

The Privilege of God means having God's heart beat in our chests for the well-being of others. It represents the privilege we all have access to, whatever our circumstances may be, to partner with God and be a blessing to someone else.

Privilege, in its traditional sense, is defined as a special right, advantage, or immunity granted or available to only a particular person or group of people. The Privilege of God, on the other hand, is accessible to every person who chooses to tap into it.

Privilege is a sensitive topic in today's culture, because it's often associated with the resentment that some people feel toward those who have more than they do. Those accused of being privileged, meanwhile, are generally unaware of how deep their advantage or privilege runs, and therefore defend themselves against accusations of benefiting from something they don't even realize they have.

Privilege manifests itself in many different ways. One way is through our tendency to leverage our advantages on behalf of those who are like us, rather than with those who are not. This is a classic example of in-group bias.

To recap, in-group bias is the often subconscious tendency to give preferential treatment to those in your in-group.

Any group in power favors its own in the media, in legal systems, in the corporate world, and whenever opportunities arise to reinforce their own positions of power. When a favored group reinforces the notion that its group members are more capable than others, the best opportunities continue to flow to those in the favored group. False stereotypes about the less favored groups develop, and are reinforced through the privileged majority's narrative. This self-perpetuating system can strengthen the prevailing power structure of a city, state, or nation for generations.

Left Out

I'm in an often overlooked minority: I'm a lefty.

If you're right-handed, you probably can't understand what it's like to live in a left-handed world. That's why I love Dr. Steven Jones's analogy of privilege and being right-handed. He asks, "Do we live in a right-handed or left-handed world?"[26]

Dr. Jones points out, "We shake hands with our right hands. We pledge with our right hand. We salute with our right hand. We take legal and governmental oaths with our right hand. School desks are set up for right-handed people. Most baseball mitts and golf clubs are designed for right-handed people. . . . Notebooks and three-ring binders are designed for right-handed people to write comfortably." Just ask a left-handed person if their left hand was stained with ink from elementary school writing lessons.

We live in a right-handed world, and the majority—the righties—don't even realize this. But every single lefty notices it, every single day.

Right-handed people come to expect doors to open a certain way—

literally and figuratively. The right-handed people are in the majority, and will therefore make decisions that benefit them. Even if a lefty is in a decision-making role, the prevailing culture of right-handedness would require the lefty to make decisions that reinforce societal norms and keep things running smoothly for the majority.

Now, switch out *right-handed people*—the in-group—for *White Americans*. Then substitute *left-handed people*—the out-group—for everyone else. Does the concept of privilege suddenly seem more plausible?

Self-Sacrificing Privilege

Standing at baggage claim while waiting for my suitcase to arrive, I continued a conversation with a lady who had been seated next to me on the plane.

When the topic of this book came up, we discussed the need for a level playing field for people of color, and the inherent advantages she had as a White woman. Her immediate response was: "I've worked hard for everything I have, and I don't feel like I have had an unfair advantage over others."

That's cool, and I didn't disagree. But there's a difference between feeling advantaged as an *individual* and possessing an advantage as a *group*. This has nothing to do with being born with a silver spoon or individual choices about how hard you work. Privilege has everything to do with circumstances that are beyond your control.

To press the issue further, I asked if she was concerned that her race would negatively impact her ability to be approved for a loan. She looked at me as if to say, *What a stupid question!* But then she took a moment to reflect on the question, and replied, "I've never thought about it. Of course my race wouldn't be an issue."

I looked back at her with a big smile. She was starting to see my point!

I then asked, "Do you ever worry that you'd be denied or discouraged from certain housing opportunities or be followed in a department store because of your race?"

Without hesitation she said, "Absolutely not."

"Have you ever thought of how your behavior in a situation could put your race on trial or be a reflection on others who share your race? In other words, do you ever think about how your actions could result in someone telling you you're a credit, or a disgrace, to your entire race?"

(Sidenote: I can't even *tell* you how many times I've been told, "You're a credit to your race." These words tell me that you must not know many people of my race. Though I'm sure it's meant to be a compliment, it's like telling someone they're "pretty for a black girl." Why can't she just be pretty? Why can't I just be awesome?)

Again, with a frown, she answered, "No."

After a long pause she added, "That's an awful lot of pressure."

Yes, the pressure is real. And my new friend was beginning to understand what so many people of color experience every single day. In search of a home in Maryland, my sister was told by the agent that she would need to find an "appropriate neighborhood" for her family—racially appropriate.

Now, was my new friend racist because she was born with advantages that come with being white? Not at all. Should she feel ashamed of being a beneficiary of these advantages? Again the answer is a resounding NO.

But on the flip side, would her denial of their existence erase them from the experiences of those who are burdened by them? Nope—not for a second. She could easily go on with her day, blissfully unaware of her advantages, while those who are negatively impacted continue to struggle against a culture that doesn't privilege them in the same way. The disconnect between one's perception of their advantages and reality makes meaningful dialogue on this issue incredibly challenging.

In an attempt to level the playing field, enormous strides have been made by civil rights leaders to secure citizenship, voting rights, and educational opportunities for people of color. In turn, previously unchallenged positions of power and privilege held by White males have been threatened. As a result, some White Americans claim that policies have gone too far and now maintain that reverse racism, or "Black privilege," is the norm. With the ever-increasing diversity of our nation, White people are feeling the pressure to accept diversity at the expense of their own power.

But the real problem—the one that everyone wants to solve but can't on their own—lies far beneath the public-policy debates that rattle on between political commentators. And the real problem can only be addressed through God's loving transformation of our hearts.

The insatiable desire to assume power for one's own benefit at the expense of others affects everyone equally: Whites, Blacks, Asians, and Latinos alike. This desire is rooted in a false understanding of the world as a zero-sum game where everything I get has to be taken from you, so that your loss is my gain. It's also rooted in selfish ambition, which directly contradicts Godly ambition.

The misguided belief that you have to take from another in order to gain for yourself stems from a humanistic view of the world. It's one in which a distant and aloof God with limited resources can't and won't provide for you. The logical conclusion of this thinking is that you have to figure out how to take care of yourself. This falsehood is contradicted throughout the Bible, but most poignantly in Philippians 4:19: "My God shall supply all your need according to His riches in glory by Christ Jesus." God's very nature is to provide for His children, and He always does. *Nothing* can prevent God from delivering every good gift He has in store for you.

The other root problem—selfish ambition—is equally prevalent in every race, culture, and group. By nature, we are selfish creatures. As children, we naturally default to the word *Mine!* long before we are socialized to share. Selfish ambition stands in stark contrast to Godly ambition, and is roundly denounced throughout the Bible. Philippians 2:3–4, in particular, advises us to "let nothing be done through selfish ambition or conceit, but in lowliness of mind let each esteem others better than himself. Let each of you look out not only for his own interests, but also for the interests of others."

Taken together, these humanistic desires drive us to search for answers where they cannot be found. We look to politics, the government, the media, the courts, and other external sources of power to fix what's broken—but none of it can.

Now don't get me wrong: I'm *not* saying that the world's efforts at leveling the playing field are bad, or go against the heart of God. I'm *incredibly* grateful for those who abolished slavery, marched for civil rights, and gave me the opportunity to participate as a full citizen in our democratic process. In fact, I believe that the people of God are called to bring justice into this world, and that equality is a worthy goal to strive for.

But I also understand why many people resent being told that they're responsible or somehow need to "pay" for the privilege they may not even be aware they were born into.

In my mind, neither blaming others nor looking to the government, media, or any other source of power can completely level the playing field. The only way we'll ever truly defeat the racial divide is through a fundamental change in our own hearts. And transformative cultural change can only happen when we replace our hearts with God's heart, by choosing the Third Option.

God's heart, which He longs to give us, is embodied in Jesus' ultimate sacrifice: the giving up of His life—and all the privilege that accompanies being God's holy and perfect Son—for us.

When we replace our hearts with God's, we'll naturally look for ways to extend our privileges and advantages to others without thinking twice about our own well-being. Because we can rest assured that God will take care of our needs, we seek to consciously rid ourselves of selfish ambition by sacrificing for others. As Jesus said in John 15:13, "Greater love has no one than this, than to lay down one's life for his friends." While I doubt you'll ever be called on to die for the sake of others, that level of sacrificial love is the standard every Christian is called to.

The Privilege of God

Defy Ventures's executive volunteers caught a glimpse of how their privilege had shaped their lives. And whether they realized it or not, they were being primed by the Privilege of God.

This new form of privilege softened their hearts, helping them realize that while they couldn't control the privilege into which they had been born, they could control what they did with it.

So now I have four questions for you.

1. Do you believe that God is fighting for you and can work out justice for you even when man gets in the way?

Everyone has their own perspective of their advantages and disadvantages in life, but the question I'm asking is this: Is God in the middle of your journey?

We live in a flawed world run by flawed people, but we have the privilege and honor to walk through that process with a perfect God. Do you believe that? Can you thank God, amidst the difficult and unfair times, for the privilege of walking with Him and for His role in your journey? The night Jesus gave His life, he was stressed to the point of sweating blood. He asked God whether there was any way to achieve His goals other than through an excruciating crucifixion. But he immediately followed up with a statement of full submission, saying, "Not My will, but Yours, be done." The only way Jesus could bring Himself to say that was because He knew and trusted His loving Father.

Are you holding on to the privilege of knowing that God is fighting for you? And do you believe that God's power is greater than any man who could ever fight against you?

Whatever your position may be in this cultural privilege war, is God the main source of your provision, joy, and enthusiasm for life? Or have you been imprisoned by your anger and resentment toward others for "keeping you" from getting what you feel you deserve?

When you think about privilege in America and the unfairness of racism, how do you respond in your heart toward others and to God? Does it make you resent Him? Have you found yourself accusing Him of being unfair? Can you acknowledge His hand in using unfairness and culture to help you become holy?

Let me encourage you by reminding you that no man can stand between you and the promises of God. Just as God was faithful to deliver Joseph—who was sold into slavery by his brothers, falsely imprisoned, to ultimately be elevated to second-in-command over all of Egypt—He will be faithful to deliver you from all unrighteousness and injustice. He proclaims in Jeremiah 29:11: "For I know the thoughts that I think toward you, says the Lord, thoughts of peace and not of evil, to give you a future and a hope." Hold on to His promise that the best is yet to come!

2. *Do you view your advantaged opportunities and achievements as blessings from God or deserved entitlements? Can you thank God and credit Him for your blessings as an act of His grace, or do you think it's something He owes you?*

Pride causes people to believe that they get what they deserve—especially when what they get is good. Pride tells us that financial success is earned and so is poverty. Pride celebrates achievement and judges failure. This mind-set is an example of just-world bias, an assumption that the world is just and fair, and therefore, people get what they deserve.

Pride will also make you believe that somehow you earned your advantages. Pride looks at others, and says "those people" have lived with their problems for generations, and they've learned to deal with it. Don't bother trying to alleviate their problems: they need to fix them on their own.

When we substitute God's privilege for ours, we stop listening to the voice of pride, and actively honor others in ways that unlock doors of opportunity for them. And if we're on the receiving side of another's privilege, we thank God for encouraging them to help us along on our journey while looking for ways to bless others with what we've received.

Now, to be clear, good decisions and hard work are absolutely critical to manifesting good outcomes. It is important for people to persevere in the face of disadvantages and honor the strength that God has given us to stay the course. God specifically calls us to "run the race" of life with perseverance. He also reminds us to do our best in everything we do "as though we were working for the Lord" (Colossians 3:23).

Pride, however, causes us to overlook the fact that we all enter the race of life at different starting points. Pride attributes our good or bad luck solely to our own efforts. This type of pride stands in opposition to the truth of God. We must replace it in our hearts so that God can reshape our perspectives on privilege.

If we do not acknowledge the grace of God in our lives, we will never appreciate God as the source of our blessings. Grace, by definition, is God's *undeserved* favor. The key word is *undeserved*. Which is to say, unearned. Can't pay for it. It's never owed to you. Grace is the opposite of works, and destroys the claims of pride.

It is also critical to remember that if blessings come from God, they can also be taken back by God. It is His prerogative to leverage grace in and through our lives any way He chooses.

I've worked hard for everything I have in this life, but I promise you that there are many who have worked twice as hard and have a fraction of what I have through no fault of their own. What, then, can I attribute my success to, other than the grace He's given me?

This is not a suggestion to settle for less but to honor the greatest source of strength and perseverance we have: the presence and promises of God.

How often do you thank Him for what you have? How often do you acknowledge that everything you have actually belongs to Him?

May I suggest that we each take a moment today to thank God for what He's given us? Walk around your house, look at your bank statements and car, and say, "Thank you, God." Thank Him for the opportunities He's given you to work, and your ability to earn wealth. Thank Him for the fact that we live in a first-world country where working and earning are even possible!

Deuteronomy 8:18 says: "And you shall remember the Lord your God, for it is He who gives you power to get wealth . . ." John 15:5 says, "Apart from Me, you can do nothing."

If you can remember that God is the source of all your provision, you are one step closer to understanding the Privilege of God.

3. *How do your blessings and advantages impact your views of yourself, compared to others?*

If you grew up with two parents, attended private school, ate breakfast every day at home, had mentors throughout your life, had your college paid for, and worked in your father's company, then good for you! Enjoy it. But does it make you feel superior? Does it make you look down on anyone else for not being able to achieve what you've achieved in life?

The truth is, you cannot blame people for what they were born into, and you cannot credit them for it, either.

Hard work is to be rewarded, but does having more than someone else make you feel superior to them? Or does having less make you feel inferior?

If you view your blessings as entitlements, you'll foster a sense of superiority over those who don't have them. This sense of superiority will drive a wedge between you and others, preventing you from loving your neighbor. It will cause you to hold on to those symbols of superiority as part of your identity when in fact they are mere expressions of God's generosity.

If, on the other hand, you view your advantages as blessings from God, they will be reasons for being not haughty, but humbled and grateful.

Do you understand or even think to ask about the burdens of those you resent for their privileges? Do you ever wonder how their families are impacted by their privileges? With every privilege comes a burden, and while it may seem like their lives are far better than yours, that may be far from the truth. I understand that it may be hard to ask God to give you compassion for those who seem to have so much more than you do, but we are called to treat everyone equally, and to love our rich brothers and sisters as much as we do the poor.

Have you developed a sense of generosity—in spite of what you lack—for someone who lacks even more than you?

Ask God to bring to mind someone you might resent for how much or how little privilege they appear to have, and ask Him to give you a heart of compassion for that person.

Ask Him to help you recognize that just as there is always someone who has more, there is always someone who has less. You may be on welfare, but someone else may be homeless. You may be struggling to feed your kids, but there's a woman out there who can't even have kids.

Recognize your blessings and ask for opportunities to encourage others through a smile, an encouraging word, and God's love.

4. In what ways do you leverage your advantages and earthly blessings to love your neighbor?

Luke 12:48 says: "When someone has been given much, much will be required in return; and when someone has been entrusted with much, even more will be required."

If you believe that God is the source of your joy and purpose, that He is the source of your blessings, and that He is the One who determines your value—however little or much you may have materially—you are truly, truly free. You're free from the bondage of false ideas of success and value. You're free from the world's determination of your worth. And, most important, you're free to possess the privilege of a heart that is focused on the purposes of God in your life.

So back to my question: How are you leveraging what you have to bless your neighbor?

First, you must identify who you view as members of your in-group and out-group. Members of both groups are your neighbors, and are to be equally honored.

Second, you should ask God to clear your heart of any anger, resentment, or jealousy you may harbor against members of your out-group.

Third, you should be free of feelings of superiority *and* inferiority. You are a child of God, made in His image, and deeply loved.

And finally, you should be free enough to say to God, "Use me to bless others!"

Accept the fact that throughout your life, there will always be a struggle for justice. I am not at all suggesting that you should cease to play a role in bringing about justice; rather, I'm suggesting that you adopt a posture of privilege that is rooted in God's love for others.

Finally, if any of these questions have challenged you, and you feel overwhelmed by all that God has asked of you, take a step back, thank God for his faithfulness in perfecting you, and remember that with God all things are possible.

Next Steps

1. In what way could you leverage your life to help someone else?

2. What attitudes in your heart would change first if you were to express the Privilege of God?

3. What type of person would be the easiest or hardest for you to leverage your advantage to help?

Prayer

For the Lord God is a sun and shield; the Lord bestows favor and honor. No good thing does He withhold from those who walk uprightly. (Psalm 84:11)

Dear God, I trust that you will open doors for me that no man can shut. I believe that You will fight my battles. I believe that my self-worth is not determined by what my critics think of me or the opportunities I do or don't get. I believe that the opportunities you give me are not only for my enjoyment but also for Your glory. I know that You bless me so that I may be a blessing to others. Transform my heart so that I can love and bless others the way You want me to.

In Jesus' name, Amen.

PART III

YOU

With the plank out of my own eye, I can begin to see you more accurately and lovingly.

Our goal in the chapters to come is to say, with more honesty and clarity, *I better understand you.*

This is only possible when we understand the burdens associated with walking in someone else's shoes.

CHAPTER 12

Honorable Assumptions

I see your color, and I assume you're a troublemaker.

"I think the members of the community need to just do what the police tell them and there won't be any problems."

"I totally disagree. The police have too much power, and the abuse of that power is the source of all the problems we see."

Ralph, a big, burly White cop, was going at it with Johnnie, an African American man in his twenties.

This sort of exchange is typical at the beginning of a "Game Changer" event. Sean Sheppard designed Game Changer events to strengthen relationships between law enforcement officers and minority communities in San Diego. He's convinced that if the two groups better understood each other, there will be less violence on the streets.

Changing the Game

The Game Changer meeting lasts three hours, and in that time the group is led through a discussion on race, police violence, and community relations. At the end of the session, there's a game. More on that in a minute.

At the start of each meeting, there's palpable tension in the room: each side with their arms crossed, ready to defend their turf, both literally and figuratively. Inevitably, over the course of three hours of listening and sharing on both sides, hearts begin to soften. But what really makes this meeting a game changer is that everyone attends a sporting event together immediately after the session.

The combination of open dialogue and quality time together has proven to be truly transformational. San Diego has seen a marked decrease in tension between communities and law enforcement officers who've participated in these meetings. That's because Sean's goal in each session is to help each side change their *own* perspectives, rather than convince the other side to change *their* opinions.

It's hard to hate someone you've really gotten to know—and just as difficult to agree with someone you don't. Sean's genius is in facilitating the "knowing"—simply getting each side to listen to the other, and giving them a reason to spend time together.

"Before" and "after" interviews on both sides speak to the success of the program. Going into a Game Changer, community leaders generally believe that police officers have too much power over their communities and that racism and police bias against people of color are obstacles to building trust.

Law enforcements' pre–Game Changer attitudes reflect a concern over their inability to communicate with communities of color, as well as the need for greater "compliance" on the part of community members. Police officers generally believe that when communities understand what their duties are, community members will be more likely to cooperate with their requests. In order for this to happen, however, there has to be an established baseline of trust, predicated on open lines of communication.

Without an established baseline of trust, neither side can address the underlying issue: a lack of honor and love for the other. Going into a Game Changer, both sides are fixated on changing the *other*, with no self-awareness as to how they *themselves* must change.

A Change of Opinion

At the conclusion of each Game Changer, a paradigm shift occurs. Both sides recognize the need for open lines of communication as a precondition for building trust, and both commit to taking proactive measures to make that happen.

In the meeting I referenced above, officers and members of the community had to talk things out face-to-face before they realized they both wanted the same thing: peace. Once they agreed on that shared outcome as their goal, they were able to engage each other with newfound understanding and respect.

Officers acknowledged their need to get out of their patrol cars and visit with community members more regularly. They also agreed to teach young officers how to communicate with greater respect.

Those in the community vowed to speak more respectfully to the police. They also agreed to post more balanced, less inflammatory comments about the officers on social media.

All of this was agreed to in a matter of hours, as a simple result of spending quality time together.

By the end of the Game Changer, Ralph and Johnnie were sitting next to each other, watching the game, talking, and laughing like old friends. They still disagreed on some things but agreed on the most important principle of all: mutual honor.

The three takeaways I gleaned from my experience with Game Changers have universal applicability, and I encourage you to internalize them as well:

First, don't give up on each other. Both the police and the community agreed that they wanted the same outcome, which they could only attain together. Naturally, this requires both time and patience, and a commitment to each other allows for both.

Second, ask yourself the hard question: Do I have honorable or dishonorable assumptions about others? If you spend time getting to know others, your assumptions will likely change, your personal attitudes toward them will most certainly improve, and the ripple effect continues outward into society. It all starts with you.

Third, commit to facilitating game-changing talks between law enforcement officers and members of your own community. We can each be game changers in our own rights by ditching finger-pointing blame and taking the time to really listen and understand what others feel and believe.

Gray Area

Mike walked up to the driver's window and asked for his license and registration.

"I ain't giving you nothin,'" a man's voice growled.

In an instant, Mike opened the door, yanked the man out of the car, and threw him onto the ground. The bruised driver was later charged with refusing to give identification to the police.

For many years Mike, a Maryland cop, held "dishonorable assumptions" about everyone he encountered on his calls. He didn't start his career with these assumptions, but they developed over years of daily battles with people. He was spit on, he was cursed at, he had rocks thrown at him, and he had been falsely accused. Over time, his attitude turned negative toward everyone he encountered. In the same way, the dishonorable assumptions toward the police were developed over time as well.

Mike couldn't show regard for others' feelings because no regard was shown for his. He assumed the worst about others, and they assumed the worst of him. This vicious cycle led to even more tension building between Mike and the neighborhood he patrolled. It got so bad that his own police station gave him the nickname "Gray Area," because he had a habit of doing whatever he could get away with. He was investigated multiple times for use of excessive force, but he never changed, because he didn't understand the impact his behavior had on instigating reciprocal dishonorable responses from the community.

Now, let me say up front that I believe people like Mike become cops to serve and protect the peace in our communities. I also know that unless we walk a mile in their shoes, we can't fully understand the pressures police officers like Mike deal with on a daily basis.

Unfortunately, Mike himself didn't realize that those daily pressures weren't legitimate excuses for abusing his power. Moreover, he truly believed that everyone he encountered was hostile and deserving of the treatment they received from him.

As the Game Changer event proved, both communities and the police want the same thing: peace. In fact, police officers are commonly referred to as "peace officers." I believe that the vast majority of law enforcement officers go to work each day for the express purpose of bringing peace to our neighborhoods. So how is it that so many are accused of bringing drama instead?

Unfortunately, one bad apple can ruin it for everyone. A community that's already on high alert only needs one bad police encounter to deepen the mistrust they are already inclined toward.

We all have a responsibility to put away the past and focus on God's calling on our lives: the call to love and honor one another. Philippians 3:13–14 says, "Forgetting what is behind and straining toward what is ahead, I press on toward the goal to win the prize for which God has called me heavenward in Christ Jesus." This principle applies to past negative experiences with ethnic groups, officers, and individuals. It is not a suggestion but a command. We are told to leave those behind and focus on our future—the future we have a hand in cocreating with God.

For those who haven't yet mastered this commandment—one of the toughest in the Bible—the repercussions are enormous. When two people don't trust each other, it's a recipe for trouble. Dishonorable assumptions always lead to dishonorable results.

In the context of police-community relations, dishonorable assumptions manifest as:

I see your color, and I assume you're a troublemaker.

You have a gun, and you intend to use it.

These assumptions stem from personal experience, the media, and the experiences of the people you know and love—your in-group. An in-group is defined as those who share your profession, race, culture, and/or perspective of the world. The opposite of an in-group is an out-group—those who don't share your profession, race, culture, or perspective of the world. And the more the "other" remains an out-group, the more readily dishonorable assumptions are reinforced and maintained.

I see your color, and I assume you have a bad attitude and could easily become violent.

What color do you assume I'm talking about?

What if it's the blue of a police uniform? Do you have negative assumptions about the color blue? Or do you have negative assumptions about people of color?

I've outlined below three dishonorable assumptions that often arise in interactions between communities of color and law enforcement. More important, I offer suggestions for turning dishonorable assumptions into honorable assumptions with honorable results.

Dishonorable Assumption #1: Their life is a recurring nightmare.
Our lives are ever-unfolding stories that involve our families, dreams, and talents. In the course of our stories, mistakes and hard times are inevitable. We all have ups and downs, good days and bad days.

This dishonorable assumption diminishes the story of the person we encounter, leading us to label them as a person with no credible dreams, just nightmares. This causes us to diminish and devalue the journey of a person God has breathed life, dreams, and hope into.

Dishonorable Assumption #2: Their story will inevitably end badly.
We all go through difficult times in our lives when a bad ending seems inevitable. But our stories aren't over till they're over, and God, who writes our endings, offers hope for the hurting.

This dishonorable assumption assumes that God can't reach into someone's life and create a happy ending. When you believe this lie, you become okay with being a part of the bad story you've made up about them in your mind. You can justify simply being a participant in the drama they "deserve," and you expect. This assumption discredits the potentially positive investment you can make in their life.

Dishonorable Assumption #3: They will not respond positively if treated respectfully.
The Golden Rule—treat others as you'd like to be treated—applies, whether you're treating people negatively or positively. Everyone wants to be treated respectfully. So it's safe to say that, as a general principle, when you treat others with respect, they'll do the same in return.

This dishonorable assumption doesn't account for the Golden Rule. Instead it looks at a group of "others" and assumes "they" operate by a different set of rules. This mind-set anticipates conflict, which sets the heart, nervous system, and mind into escalation mode. A fight-or-flight response ensues, leading you to assume you'll need to overpower them. Your mind literally tells your body, *I'll need to meet force with more force in order to survive.*

Working backward, if you predetermine in your mind that an encounter will turn violent, how do you think that conversation will begin? I understand that police, and those they encounter, must always prepare for the worst. But sometimes dishonorable assumptions become a self-fulfilling prophecy.

Those who operate under this assumption communicate disrespectfully and forcefully to control a situation. For Officer Mike, his choice to act forcefully was based on a series of self-fulfilling, dishonoring assumptions. He became jaded and developed an "us"-versus-"them" mentality. In other words, he was no longer serving the community to help bring peace; he was perpetuating his own assumptions and making situations worse.

The Assumption Challenge

Officer Mike was called in one day by his commander and told to go into the very community that gave him the most angst—the one where people threw rocks at him, spat on him, and called him "Uncle Tom" because he was a Black officer. He was ordered to start talking with people and build better relationships between the police and the community. Officer Mike argued that the Black neighborhood was a lost cause and that it would never work.

His commander sent him in anyway. Reluctantly, with no expectation that any good would come of it, he and another officer went in and simply started talking to people. They began with the teenagers, since they were the source of most of the crime and violence.

Officer Mike talked to them about their lives, their struggles, and what they needed in the community. The teenagers told them that the recreation center was rarely open and they simply wanted to play basketball there. Mike agreed to help get it opened more often, but with one catch. They needed to resolve the issue together. So together they contacted the recreation department, which agreed to extend their operating hours.

Most crimes and calls about drug dealing were happening on Friday and Saturday nights. So, from 10:00 p.m. to 1:00 a.m. on those nights, Mike and other officers opened the center for "midnight basketball" and provided pizza. From this seemingly simple act there was an immediate reduction in violent crime and calls for service in that neighborhood.

The officers kept listening and responding. These first steps turned into barbecues with the kids and their parents and, eventually, the entire community. Those barbecues turned into weekly meetings where Officer Mike mentored kids and helped them prepare for job interviews. He even approached local businesses and asked them for help in getting these kids jobs, which they agreed to do. The teens who'd been so troublesome before began confiding in Mike and asking his advice for their lives.

None of this would have happened without Officer Mike's eventual and reluctant decision to embrace the Third Option. By stepping out of the "gray area," talking to people, and building relationships, Officer Mike showed his willingness to engage with the community, and a significant transformation occurred. Mike's out-group became his in-group, and along with that came honorable assumptions (or in-group bias). As assumptions on both sides began to shift, crime went down, and Officer Mike became the peace officer he always wanted to be.

Making the Shift

Turning dishonorable assumptions into honorable ones requires an affirmative decision to pursue the Third Option. Here are some honorable assumptions we can adopt to displace dishonorable ones in our hearts.

Honorable Assumption #1: That person's life is an unfolding story that God is still working on.

Do you believe that life is a downward spiral, or do you believe that the best is yet to come—in your own life and in the lives of others?

We're all on a journey, discovering and fulfilling our purpose. As God says in Jeremiah 29:11, "I know the plans I have for you—plans to prosper you, to give you a hope and a future."

When we interact with someone, we can choose to see them as a fellow traveler on the same journey toward a brighter future. We can choose to learn about their journey and realize that, though their experience may look different than ours, the ups and downs we all go through are very similar.

When we do this, we become a positive part of that person's story. We honor God and our neighbors when we place ourselves in their shoes, helping them realize God's best outcome for their lives—and ours.

Honorable Assumption #2: They want their story to end positively.

In our heart of hearts, everyone wants to live a productive, fulfilling life. Everyone wants to develop their talents, be valued and loved, and be successful at something. Even if their actions and words express defeat, deep inside there's a flicker of hope that can be ignited with one kind word or opportunity. Proverbs 13:12 says, "Hope deferred makes the heart sick, but when the desire comes, it is a tree of life."

Every person has a hope for something better in their life—a hope that waits for an opportunity to be fulfilled or encouraged. By assuming that God is writing a positive ending to each person's story, we open our hearts up to the possibility that we can play a role in turning their story around. We become sensitive to their emotional, spiritual, and practical needs, and help them feel loved, valued, and purposeful.

Honorable Assumption #3: They will respond positively if I communicate honorably.

Because we're designed to live in loving, positive relationships, any communication that expresses honor will be received more positively than communication that's dishonoring. As Proverbs 15:1 says, "A soft answer turns away wrath, but a harsh word stirs up anger."

When Officer Mike was ordered to build relationships with kids he'd had conflict with, he was skeptical. But he quickly learned the power of treating others with honor. Their relationships improved so much that when Officer Mike got promoted and moved to a different part of town, the kids he'd mentored tracked him down—after they graduated, landed a good job, got married, and had kids. A few even asked Mike to be the godfather of their children. And some, once out of jail, even thanked him for sending them there.

Honorable assumptions lead to honorable results. As the Bible says, "Love is patient, love is kind, it is not proud, it does not dishonor others, it is not self-seeking, it is not easily angered, it keeps no record of wrongs. Love does not delight in evil but rejoices with the truth. It always protects, always trusts, always hopes, always perseveres" (1 Corinthians 13:4–7). Or, in the words of Maya Angelou, "Love recognizes no barriers. It jumps, hurdles, leaps fences, penetrates walls to arrive at its destination full of hope."

Honorable assumptions flow naturally from choosing the Third Option. By aligning our hearts with God's, we become people who embrace honor and hope over disdain and frustration.

The Color of Hope

I recently had the honor of interviewing an officer with the St. Louis County Police Department. The city of Ferguson is located in St. Louis County, and the officer I interviewed was on the front lines of the protests that erupted after the shooting of Michael Brown. We spoke for an hour, and what he said gave me hope that healing can happen.

On the one-year anniversary of the shooting, there was a national call to protest in front of the Ferguson Police Department. This officer was ordered to stand on guard in the front of the building. He told me about the images that stood out from those weeks of protests and meetings:

> I have two pictures resulting from those weeks of protests and meetings. The first includes me, a large crowd, and two young people yelling right in my face. The passion on the faces of the young man and woman were clear.
>
> Several weeks later I was attending a community meeting led by David Anderson. The meeting was a little contentious. There was some disagreement, but it was a healthy disagreement. A comment was made about police brutality, and somebody asked me, "Have you ever seen police brutality?" I answered no, and was called a liar.
>
> During a break, I showed John, one of the facilitators, the photo on my phone, and he said, "Hey, those two people are sitting right over there!"
>
> I went over and introduced myself to them, showed them the photo, and grinned. "I'm pretty sure this is you," I said.
>
> They laughed, but were also struck by the image. "Yeah, that was me," [one] said. And we started talking about it. When the meeting ended, I went over and I asked if I could take another picture. This one showed us all together, with a much different feeling.

Don't get me wrong. We didn't become best friends that night, but to me it was hopeful. In subsequent conversations with the young man, I learned so much about his experience with the police. I also found out this young man, and his brother, were both assaulted by a police officer.

If we say, as law enforcement, that we will not tolerate inappropriate behavior, inappropriate social media, police brutality, racial profiling, then we have to be transparent and address it appropriately. If people don't believe that the agency is policing itself, even if they do come and approach the agency, they feel like their concerns aren't valued. Their complaints aren't investigated and nothing changes.

Two Minutes of Honor

The officer continued. . . .

When you're a young policeman, the thirty-second interaction you have with a citizen has more of an impact than you will ever know. The way you interact with somebody, even if it's for two minutes, is going to leave an impression on that person about the profession as a whole. And so your snide comment, being cynical, blowing somebody off instead of saying hi, or taking a moment to wave at a little girl when she waves at you—all of those little things leave a lasting impression, for better or worse.

For example, I'm a young policeman working in the south area of St. Louis County, and I came across two young boys. I just rolled my window down and introduced myself. "Hey, guys, how are you? You guys live here?" To me it was just a polite thing to do.

I talked to them for a few minutes, got to know their names, and drove on by. A week later, we talked again. In about three weeks I met their father. He says, "Hey, my boys say they know you. If we have any problems, is it okay for them to call you?" I said it was no problem. I had worked in that precinct for about four years.

Five years go by, and I take my boys to baseball practice one day. Guess who is at the practice as a coach? It's the father, and one of his kids is also helping coach. Through our kids, we became really good friends.

Our friendship started with a minor act: I just drove through an apartment complex with my window down, talking to the young men I came across. I didn't think much of it at the time, but I can see now how it all started with an honorable assumption and treating these kids like they were my own.

This officer turned an honorable assumption into a lifelong friendship, with far-reaching consequences for the neighborhood he patrolled. Imagine the impact you and I could have by simply taking a page from his playbook and proactively applying honorable assumptions to everyone we meet.

Next Steps

1. Can you name a dishonorable assumption someone has about you and how it made you feel?

2. Can you name a dishonorable assumption you have about someone or a group of people and think about why you have that assumption about them?

3. The next time you encounter someone who looks differently than you, ask yourself if your assumptions about them are honorable or dishonorable. Are you thinking the worst or the best? Do you want to be a part of the sad or happy ending to their story? If

you are harboring dishonorable assumptions, offer positive verbal encouragement to them and see how it changes how you feel about them in your heart.

Prayer

"Judge not, that you be not judged. For with what judgment you judge, you will be judged; and with the measure you use, it will be measured back to you." (Matthew 7:1–2)

Lord, reveal to me the thoughts and intents of my heart toward people. Challenge me to hold honorable assumptions about individuals and groups, especially those with whom I have little interaction and know little about. Give me the courage to choose the Third Option, by taking the first step toward acting honorably.

In Your name I pray, Amen.

CHAPTER 13

Color-Coded Pain

Would I stand out? Would I be approached by anyone?

Everyone, regardless of their color, suffers pain of some sort. This is the reality of our fallen world. But this chapter narrows our focus on a few of the ways that minorities in America are disproportionately burdened by being the "other."

One of the five people I asked to conduct the "Walk in My Shoes" field trip visited an African American church. Courtney is a thirty-two-year-old White woman from Michigan. Here's her account of the experience, in her own words.

What you did you feel emotionally?
My initial emotional reaction was nervousness and uncertainty.

Initial thoughts about what would or could happen?
My main thoughts were *I won't fit in; they will wonder why I'm there and might think that I think I'm better than them.*

As I reflected on those thoughts, I realized how self-centered they were. I was projecting thoughts that may never come to fruition. I felt nervous that I would offend someone with my actions or statements.

Describe your emotions and thoughts while driving to the location.

On my way to the church, I wondered if I would be greeted. Would I stand out? Would I be approached by anyone? Would I come across as sincere? Would I be asked to do something I didn't feel comfortable doing? Would I enjoy the worship experience and teaching?

Describe the location you went to.

I went to a church with roughly one hundred people, and every person was African American.

Describe your emotions upon arrival.

I was nervous about whom I would interact with. I felt uneasy entering the church but also anxious to see what I would learn about myself.

Being the "Other" Is Stressful

I felt a lot of anxiety in Courtney's answers. How about you?

There's a lot of stress related to being the "other." For people of color, being an "other" is a daily reality in America. It can cause so much stress that it can negatively impact your physical and mental well-being. Courtney's experience of being the "other" for two hours is one small but powerful illustration.

Even though we can never really know what it's like to walk in someone else's shoes, sometimes all it takes is a glimpse into their world to touch our hearts. The better we understand the burden others carry, the easier it is to honor their pain, and the more likely we'll be to try and alleviate it.

This motivation to learn is not necessarily due to individual guilt or fault. We seek to understand others based on honor for the image of God in them. We honor others by acknowledging their plight and allowing ourselves to experience a little discomfort in an effort to understand them.

I have officiated at dozens of funerals in my life, and at every single one of them I offered condolences for the pain experienced by the family. Obviously, I wasn't responsible for any of those deaths, but in each case I said, "I am sorry for your loss." And in each case I sincerely meant those words.

It's tempting to think that a book like this, especially this chapter, is written to make certain people—specifically White people—feel guilty. Nothing could be further from the truth. This book isn't about guilt, but rather encouragement for people of all ethnicities to be compassionate and understanding of those who experience a different reality.

One day, I was discussing my feeling of being the "other" with a friend. She listened for a while and asked me why I couldn't just "get over it." I explained to her that you can't just *get over it* because it's in your face all the time. There's no escaping it, and unless you've experienced being a person of color in America, you can't relate. Then it hit me to ask her, "What if you went to a place where you were the only White person?"

This question was the genesis of the first field trip. I wanted my friends to get a small taste of what people of color experience every day. And from the comments they submitted, it worked: every one of them conveyed the significant levels of stress they experienced when they were the "other." One of the respondents even joked that I should take his blood pressure before and after the field trip. The stress was real.

Race-related stress is a health hazard. There are multiple scientific studies, and even a test, that affirm it.

On My Heart

If you know your blood pressure and cholesterol levels, you can take an online assessment for atherosclerotic cardiovascular disease (ASCVD).[27]

I went to the website, indicated my gender, age, cholesterol, and race. The results declared that I had a 5.6 percent chance for cardiovascular disease. Then I went back and changed only one answer: I changed my race from Black to White. Correspondingly, my statistical likelihood for heart disease went down to 4.1 percent. In other words, I have a higher chance of cardiovascular disease just because I'm Black. The American College of Cardiology and the American Heart Association both concur that there's a connection between heart disease risk and race. But why?

One factor proposed by Dr. Rodney G. Hood is the increased allostatic load due to race-related stress on the heart and other organs of people of color. Environmental factors such as poverty, violence, poor employment, and discrimination can all stimulate physiological stress responses and release stress hormones, which raise blood pressure levels.

In America, Asians, Latinos, and Blacks have poverty rates that exceed that of Whites. In 2015, the poverty rate for Whites was 9.3 percent; Asians, 11.4 percent; Latinos, 21.4 percent; and Blacks, 24.1 percent. Poverty-related stress is a primary cause of physical and mental stress, and, based on these statistics, negatively affects minorities up to 2.5 times more than Whites.

Poor people live in lower-income neighborhoods, where a prevalence of sociological and neurological stressors include high population density, noise, crime, pollution, and discrimination, to name a few. Moreover, there are fewer resources to alleviate these pervasive stressors.

Chronic poverty-related stress causes the brain to work overtime in an attempt to mitigate stress, causing neurological damage, physical and mental disorders, and psychological problems, including depression, anxiety, and substance abuse. These impacts have a ripple effect—first within the family, then outward into the community. For those born into these circumstances, it's even harder to find a way out, because this is the only reality they've ever experienced.

What Could a World Free of Racism Feel Like?

We enjoy vacations, because they represent a place or experience associated with low stress. A vacation is spent at a place where the food is good, the people are friendly, and the environment is peaceful. There's no mental or social stress, which makes taking a vacation a life-giving experience.

After a vacation, we feel more alive, rested, optimistic, and happy. But most of us dread coming back to the "real world." If you're White, imagine if you returned from vacation and walked back into a world where the stress of being the only White person at your job, your school, your neighborhood, and every other social environment was a daily reality. You might be tempted to never return!

Going back to Courtney's account of her field trip, did you connect with her emotions of uncertainty and nervousness? Did you recognize her experience as one that highlights the stressors of *daily* life for people of color?

Talking about race-related stress shouldn't be minimized as complaining or making excuses. This is not about getting pity or blaming anyone for things that simply are. I am merely highlighting it, because race-related stress associated with being the "other" is something we must all acknowledge if we want to put an end to racism, or even outgroup discrimination.

Everyone faces their own challenges, regardless of their color.

Racial stress isn't necessarily more burdensome than all the other stresses we experience in life. But it *is* something that people of color cannot mitigate or escape, and it must be acknowledged for the effect it has on our society as a whole.

Microaggressions

You hear a lot about racial "microaggressions." This term is often associated with oversensitivity on the impacted party and is used offensively to label people as racists. The term has gotten a bad rap as a result of its misuse.

Microaggressions are brief verbal and behavioral offenses that communicate hostile, derogatory, or negative attitudes toward people of color. Perpetrators of microaggressions are often unaware that they engage in such communications when they interact with people of different racial or ethnic backgrounds. People of any color can be perpetrators of microaggressions.

Microaggressions come in the form of micro-insults, micro-invalidations, and micro-assaults.

Micro-Insults

Micro-insults are insensitive words and actions that demean a person's identity or racial heritage.

When an employee of color is asked, *How did you get your job?* someone could be asking, literally, how they got the job. Or they could be implying that people of color are not qualified and that, as a minority, they must have obtained the position through some sort of preferential quota. There may be no difference in the words they use, but the underlying intent is as different as night and day. And obviously, if it's the latter intent, that constitutes a micro-insult. The Third Option offers both parties room for honest, transparent dialogue while being aware of the trip wires.

Another example of a micro-insult is the story I mentioned in Chapter 10 when I asked a White friend to go on my now-(in)famous field trip. He automatically associated the trip with going to a dangerous neighborhood, and came up with a bunch of reasons why he couldn't. My only request was to have him go to a place where he'd be the only White person. I never told him to go to any specific neighborhood. He could have gone anywhere, but in his mind *danger* and *people of color* were synonymous—even in an African American church. By expressing his concern out loud, he uttered a micro-insult—evidenced by the other person in the conversation, who happened to be White, telling my friend that his rhetoric was offensive.

Micro-Invalidations

Micro-invalidations exclude and diminish the opinions, emotions, and experiences of another person.

When Asian Americans are told they speak "good English," it can invalidate their belonging and make them feel excluded from mainstream America.

When people are told, "I don't see color," the unintended effect of these words is to negate the significance, pain, joy, and frustration of their experiences as people of color. I've personally experienced frustration when my well-meaning friends rush to reassure me that they are "good" with Black people by saying "I don't see color." All that says to me is that they don't want to hear what I have to say and that my experience shouldn't have any impact on their actions, because they're already "good." Words like these shut down lines of communication, because they prevent real growth and understanding from taking place.

Many people are so afraid of being associated with racism that they won't allow deeper conversations about race to take place. This unwillingness to share and listen invalidates the opinions and experiences of people of color.

Micro-Assaults

Micro-assaults are overtly racist remarks occurring on an individual basis. The purpose of a micro-assault is to hurt the intended victim through name-calling, avoidant behavior, or purposefully discriminatory actions.

A perfect example of a micro-assault occurred in January 2018 during a tennis match between a Black player named John Wilson IV, who attends a historically Black university, and a White player named Spencer Brown, who attends Appalachian State. Over the course of their match, Brown made numerous racist comments toward Wilson, including "At least I know my dad." To make things worse, the Appalachian State tennis coach responded to the outrage over Brown's comments with the defensive statement, "We have a Black guy on our team," implying that because they had a Black player on their team, they couldn't possibly be racist.

Brown was immediately suspended from the team. However, the micro-assault's impact negatively affected all parties involved.

Macro-Impact

Whether conscious or unconscious, micro-aggressions are expressions of a negative view of people and communities based on color. Even though these words and actions are "micro" in nature, their compound effect over the years—on society and these communities in particular— have taken their toll.

But back to my field trip invitations for a moment: nothing I suggested specified a "dangerous neighborhood" but simply a place to be the "other." As already mentioned, his mind automatically went to the worst-case scenario, resulting in a barrage of negative comments about people of color. Not only was this offensive, but the tendency to immediately think the worst of a group of people is a non-starter in nurturing honorable relationships—and this has long-term ramifications.

When people in authority think this way, can you imagine the efforts they will make to ensure that they never become the "other?" As we've witnessed throughout history, people will go to enormous lengths to preserve their power—as a means of either self-preservation or self-defense.

One example I mentioned earlier in this book is redlining. Redlining was one of many political tactics used in the banking industry to limit home loans to minorities. This national policy, while in effect, made it more difficult for people of color to build wealth through real estate. The people of color who were approved for home loans were limited to neighborhoods where value grew more slowly or declined. For many, this was a root cause of generational poverty.

As recently as 2015, the US Department of Housing and Urban Development (HUD) discovered that a bank in the Midwest had disproportionately denied qualified loan applicants in predominantly minority neighborhoods, compared to other lenders operating in the same communities. Thankfully, this bank stood out as an aberration, and redlining has long been outlawed. Nevertheless, it's shocking that, in this day and age, some bad actors still seek to deny access to qualified families of color simply because they live in minority neighborhoods. [28]

Does the fact that discriminatory practices still occur mean that people of color can't attain wealth in real estate? Not at all. I'm simply pointing out that the unjust burdens borne by minorities can be exacerbated by racially charged policies and practices. And while most of these policies and practices have been outlawed, discriminatory mentalities still exist today.

Painfully Poor Education

One policy area that disadvantages students of color is inequality in education. As former UN secretary-general Kofi Annan said, "Education
is the great equalizer of our time. It gives hope to the hopeless, and creates chances for those without."

Schools in lower income areas—often communities of color—have
access to less funding, due to a lower tax base and marginalized political
representation.

Schools that don't receive adequate funding put students at a disadvantage with the most inexperienced and lowest-paid teachers, limited
access to quality teaching materials, limited access to relevant technologies and new computers, and poorly equipped science labs.

Poorer schools don't have the ability to spend resources on the latest safety and security measures; cleanliness of hallways, classrooms,
and bathrooms; and maintenance issues such as broken lights, leaky
roofs, graffiti, and chipped paint.[29]

As in life, the "little" things add up to significantly disadvantage minority students.

The Pain of Incarceration

Much has been said about the need for criminal justice reform, but
nothing highlights this need better than the statistics themselves:

❖ Black drivers are three times more likely to have their cars
searched than White drivers.

❖ Black people are arrested for drug crimes at twice the rates of Whites, despite the fact that Whites use drugs at comparable rates and sell drugs at comparable or higher rates.

❖ Black Americans are more likely to be jailed while awaiting trial, because Black dependents are less able to afford to pay bail. The temporary incarceration stigmatizes the defendant, disrupts family life and employment, and makes it harder for the defendant to prepare a defense.

❖ Black defendants are 13 percent more likely to be offered plea deals that include prison time than Whites or non-Black minorities.

❖ Black men's sentences are, on average, 10 percent longer than those of their White peers, in part because prosecutors are twice as likely to file charges that carry mandatory minimum sentences against Blacks than against Whites.[30]

Based on research done by Devah Pager, professor of sociology and public policy at Harvard, a White male with a criminal record would get just as many callbacks in response to a job interview as a Black male without a criminal record. Think about that. A White male with a criminal record is just as employable as a Black male without one.[31]

As I was describing these findings to a White friend, he asked, "Do you *not* think all those people in prison are guilty?"

"I obviously can't vouch for every single one of them," I said, "but of the countless African Americans sentenced to prison in the last fifty years, many never had a fair trial."

"Never had a fair trial?" he yelled. "That's impossible in this country!"

Being arrested, put in jail, and charged with a crime is a frightening experience, especially for people whose experience with law enforcement is tainted. Many accept a plea bargain out of fear of mandatory minimum sentencing or a biased jury.

These fears are far from unfounded. Mandatory minimum sentencing laws have sent offenders away for five to ten years for first-time, low-level drug offenses. And statistics show that when a Black defendant faces an all-White jury, they are convicted 16 percent more often than whites.[32]

The fear of spending a decade in prison leads many to accept a plea bargain for shorter prison time. But this also means accepting a lifetime label of *felon*, which comes with its own burdens and renders individuals nearly unemployable. Black men have been convicted of drug charges at rates of up to fifty times higher than White men. But according to the National Institute on Drug Abuse, White students use cocaine seven times more, heroin seven times more, and crack eight times more than Black students.[33]

Being a felon all but strips individuals of many of their rights as citizens. Felons experience limitations on voting rights and jury service, are limited in gainful employment opportunities, have limited access to school loans, and have limited access to business loans. These vary from state to state.

After explaining some of these points, my friend paused and said, "You know, a friend of ours has a son who probably should be in jail for life because of things he's done. But because his dad made a phone call to a friend with the right connections, his son is sitting at home rather than in jail."

Of course, these scenarios are not always based on race. Socioeconomics have a lot to do with the cycle of pain and one's inability to take full advantage of the rights afforded in our criminal justice system. But because socioeconomic status and race are so interrelated in America, those who suffer the most are generally people of color.

In light of these facts, how honorable would it be to look past the criminal record box checked on a job application, and give consideration to applicants that have paid their debts to society and now have a need to provide for themselves and their families? The image of God in them is in no way scarred or diminished because of their past. If that were so, we would all be disqualified.

Why Can't You Get Past the Pain?

A man bought a very large fish tank and installed a piece of glass in the middle, dividing one side from the other. He placed a group of fish on one side of the glass but no fish on the other side.

At first, the fish kept bumping into the glass because they didn't see it or expect a barrier to be there. After a few painful days of head butting, the fish became conditioned to stop swimming near the invisible barrier.

Then the owner removed the glass divider. But still no fish swam past the middle of the tank.

When you've been swimming into glass your whole life, and all your friends and family tell you about the glass they've hit their heads on, you'll probably give up trying to swim past it. Similarly, when you live with constant reminders that a majority of people are scared of people who look like you, and no one cares to hear about your experiences in life, more often than not the pain prevents you from trying to change things for the better.

Can you understand now why hurting people are so desperate to experience and receive your honor?

Beautiful Realities of Honor

Here's the rest of Courtney's field trip report, which speaks to the culture of honor she willingly stepped into.

Were any comments made to or about you?

I was greeted at the front door with a handshake. Upon entering, I was greeted again by two friendly ladies. There were only about twenty people in the church when I arrived. I sat a few rows back on the side. Four people approached me and shook my hand.

A lady named Ebony introduced herself and asked how I found out about the church. I told her I was driving around and found it as my husband and I just moved to town. We talked briefly, and she was very welcoming. I later learned she was the pastor's wife.

As the service began, more people started to come in, and I noticed I was still the only White person. I have been to four different churches over the past four weeks, and this was by far the most spirit-filled and welcoming environment.

At one point, the pastor talked about the division in our nation (referring to race) and even identified the challenges of being a Black man.

I wondered, *Do people see me as the enemy? Has anyone in this room been offended by a White person? Do I represent all White people?*

We were encouraged to say hello to those around us and even hug one another. I was embraced by at least eight people during that time. After the service, I shook the hand of the greeter and walked back to my car.

How were you treated? Be specific.

I was welcomed with open arms and love. I was very humbled by the experience, but also encouraged, as this is what church should be for anyone who enters.

Here is Courtney's summary:

I love people. I love other cultures. I am intrigued by how others were raised and how their life experiences shaped them into the people they are now. I am thankful I live in an environment where I get to work and live life with people of different races and ethnicities.

Overall, I reflected on today and wondered if I have hurt someone of another race in a comment I made or something I did unconsciously. It caused me to stop and ask for forgiveness from God. I would never want someone to feel that way by me.

Like Courtney, you too can step into the shoes of the "others" and be unexpectedly blessed. There is so much that God wants to teach you about the lives and experiences of your brothers and sisters—things that you can only learn when you take the time to listen, observe, and participate in their lives, on their terms.

Next Steps

1. Can you identify a form of glass in your fish tank that serves as an invisible racial barrier you keep bumping up against?

2. Can you identify a micro-insult that you have a habit of giving or receiving? If you are the giver of them, ask a friend to hold you accountable to stop. If you are a receiver, confront the perpetrator in truth, with love.

3. Take the "discover your risk" survey for cardiovascular disease and switch up your race to see how that changes your outcome: http://tools.acc.org/ascvd-risk-estimator/.

Prayer

"Therefore, in all things [Jesus] had to be made like His brethren, that He might be a merciful and faithful High Priest in things pertaining to God, to make propitiation for the sins of the people." (Hebrews 2:17)

Dear God, I acknowledge that being uncomfortable for the sake of someone else is part of choosing the Third Option. Make me willing to be all things to all people and walk in their shoes. Help me see and better understand the pain that racism causes, and show me how to bring honor into every situation. Help me view every day as a "field trip" opportunity to learn from others. Please reveal to me the blind spots that prevent me from seeing life from the perspective of others, whether they are better or worse off than me. Please don't allow my partial knowledge or ignorance to cloud my ability to honor others, as I should.

In Jesus' name I pray, Amen.

CHAPTER 14

Full-Color Conversations

Some seem to think you're upset about something.
If you are, let's talk about it.

An interracial couple came back to visit my wife and me after a church service one Sunday. As we sat down to talk, I tried to figure out what nationality she was. Normally I ask, *Where's your family from?*

Depending on the answer, I might continue the conversation with *How many languages do you speak?* and *Teach me to say* hello *in your language.* (By the way, that line of questioning can be offensive if not done respectfully.)

(I can't tell you how many thousands of times people from all over the world have walked up to me and asked, "What *are* you?" Countless ethnic groups have claimed me as theirs and said to me, "You look like my brother or cousin." Anyway, back to my story.)

I tried to piece this woman's genetic puzzle together in my mind. Her hair was dark and straight but somewhat thick and course. She was a little darker-skinned than me, but had a slight Asian tilt to her eyes. I thought, *Maybe she is Blasian* [a Black and Asian mix]. *Or maybe Black-Apino* [Black and Filipino].

For some reason, I never got around to asking about her race in that meeting, but that didn't keep me from thinking about it. As soon as she left the room, my wife and I looked at each other with a smile and asked, "What do you think she is?"

Even though we never asked her what her nationality was, we had a conversation about race in our heads the whole time we talked with her. The truth is, we all have race conversations all the time, but if they stay in our heads, they'll never be productive.

Silence Is Not Golden

When it comes to addressing racism in America, not enough is said, so not enough is done.

A lack of interracial dialogue about racism prevents real change from happening. On the flip side, a meaningful conversation about racism is a critical starting point for a solution. If people of different ethnicities can learn to honorably communicate with and about themselves and each other, we can all move toward unity.

What is a meaningful conversation? I suggest it's a dialogue in which all participants grow and learn a different facet of the truth. If you're not seeing new truths from different perspectives, you're probably not having a meaningful conversation. A meaningful conversation occurs when two people stop trying to talk each other into their point of view and a *third* truth emerges for both parties.

Most of us prefer our current perception to that of another. After all, who doesn't like their own handiwork? But the truth is usually somewhere in the middle of two or more schools of thought.

Choosing the Third Option emboldens us to engage in real, truth-seeking dialogue with those who don't look like us. Here are seven keys to encourage and embolden you to initiate honoring conversations about race.

Key #1: Acknowledge the reality that you're always having a race conversation in your head.

The entire time I tried to figure out what nationality the woman was, I was having a race conversation in my head.

Every time you speak to, look at, or communicate with another human being, you're thinking, challenging, affirming, or expanding your views on race. When you see someone, whether they look like you or not, you're having a race conversation in your mind. You're forming and reinforcing perceptions, stereotypes, positive feelings, and fears about people—whether they look like you or not.

Pay attention to your reactions to news pertaining to Blacks, Whites, Latinos, and Asians. Consider speaking them out loud rather than keeping them in your head; after all, they'll come out of your mouth or manifest in your actions eventually. As Jesus said in Luke 6:45: "Out of the abundance of the heart [the] mouth speaks."

Now imagine your *internal* views about race being expressed verbally or publicly, e.g., on social media. Which thoughts of yours would sound shockingly offensive—and racist? Pay attention to them, but don't fret if they do. You're not alone, and we've all got a lot of growing to do in this regard. In order to grow, we must acknowledge and learn from our internal race conversations.

In our attempts to honor others, the least effective conversations will take place in our own minds. The second least effective conversations are those we have with people who hold similar views. If the only people we speak with are ourselves and those who share similar life experiences and perspectives, we're not allowing our perceptions to be challenged.

Key #2: The race conversation in your head will not stay there.

Here's an example of the power of a meaningful conversation, and the danger of not having them, from my friend Dan's perspective:

I was hired into a law firm that was basically Irish. All the marquee names were Irish surnames. The firm was very proud of its culture.

I was the first African American hired. Some years later, they hired a young Black woman. We'd see each other occasionally but rarely interacted.

A few months after she joined the firm, I started hearing talk among some of the partners. "She seems to be angry all the time." And: "She's not approachable, not the type of person you'd want to have a beer with."

I remember an associate, a junior lawyer, asking if I'd talk to her. I thought, *What am I going to talk to her about?* I felt very awkward talking with someone who didn't work with me, and even more uncomfortable that he asked me just because I'm Black. What he didn't realize was, even though we were both African American, we came from two different worlds. I grew up in an LA ghetto. She grew up in a more affluent environment and had an Ivy League education.

I pushed back at the idea of talking to her but eventually agreed. I wanted to be part of the solution. Awkwardly, I talked to her about the perceived disconnect between her and some of the partners. I offered the probability that they simply didn't understand how to communicate with people from different backgrounds. Then I added, "Some seem to think you're upset about something. If you are, let's talk about it."

She replied, "Heck no, Dan, nothing happened." Then she confided something interesting. She was taught that when you're in a group of White men, the best way to talk is to be very brief and to the point, with no extraneous discussion.

Her understanding and effort to be respectful was misperceived as being unhappy.

Clearly, the law partners and this woman weren't on the same page—or even in the same universe! They couldn't pick up on her communication style, and she couldn't pick up on theirs. On top of all that was the hovering tension over race. Both parties were having animated, presumptive, one-sided conversations about race in their own heads. Until an actual conversation was initiated, both sides operated under false assumptions regarding the other.

Consider your own preconceptions of race. Are they honoring or dishonoring? Do they presume best intentions on another's part and enable you to interact with others as equals? If not, how are they preventing you from having a meaningful conversation with someone from a different race?

The woman and her law partners all had blind spots that prevented them from engaging in meaningful conversations with each other. Their preconceived notions of each other affected their relationship in nonverbal ways, which actually spoke volumes.

What messages do *you* believe about those of your out-group? Whatever they are, they're probably misguided and incomplete, especially if your perceptions were formed only by people who look like you and share your background.

Honor people by talking *to* them and not *around* them. I know it can be awkward at first, but the benefits far outweigh the risks.

Key #3: *Honor others by allowing them to self-disclose.*
Zachary, a Black teenager, went to his high school football team's game in a White neighborhood. Somehow he found himself sitting in the bleachers on the "wrong" side of the field. A White teenage girl looked at him and asked, "Um, do you have a knife?"

"Why would I have a knife?"

"Well, I thought all of you had knives."

"No. And as a matter of fact, I don't have any friends who carry knives."

Whatever your color may be, it's honorable to listen to others disclose their opinions about you and your ethnicity. It may be tempting to write them off as ignorant, but by honoring their honesty, you can seize on an opportunity to set things straight and engage in further dialogue.

Personally, I hear this statement a lot: "You're not *really* black." Well, I may not be the Black you had in your mind, but I'm Black. This comment is often uttered by someone who's had limited interaction with Black people and has applied that limited information to the entire race. I may not always like hearing it, but I'm happy to seize on the opportunity to educate those who are less attuned in to the nuances of being Black.

If you've said something like this, ask yourself how many people in that race you really know. Not just people you've met, but actually know and have spent time with—people you'd call friends. If the answer is *very few*, you have a lot of room to learn. Let others self-disclose to you who *they* are rather than projecting *your* limited perspective onto *them*.

In the above examples, people are self-disclosing, expressing their inward thoughts and feelings. And throughout this process, if there's an honorable two-way dialogue, people are learning and relearning what they thought they knew. That's a good thing, even when it's frustrating or offensive at first. As with most things in life, *no pain, no gain*.

Meaningful encounters mess with internal social narratives and prejudices in the best possible way. Instead of only projecting our beliefs, we're listening and learning from others. I encourage you to learn about others based on what they disclose. Don't judge, but seek to establish open and honest lines of communication. Be willing to listen, forgive, and admit to mistakes. And be willing to help others learn.

Key #4: *Take every opportunity to enlighten.*

During a road trip with my college football team, a White teammate and I talked about where we grew up. As I described the front lawn of my home and the swimming pool in the backyard, his eyes widened and his eyebrows scrunched. He said, "It's like a regular neighborhood."

He assumed I had lived in an apartment building, as he thought most Black people did. He was educated by our conversation, and I had an opportunity to teach.

Now, if you're a minority in this country, you're probably asking this question: *Why do I always have to educate them about us? I'm tired of it!* I totally understand. It's discouraging when it seems like situations and perspectives never change. But I've changed, and I've seen countless others change, when we choose to honor others by enlightening them.

Proverbs 10:12 says, "Hatred stirs up strife, but love covers all sins."

If I focus on perceived negative questions, and ascribe ill intent to them, anger and frustration arise in my heart. But if I focus on the love God has given me to overwhelm negativity, no matter what the underlying motivation of the questioner may be, I can still choose to please God by honoring them rather than feeding my ego. After all, my perception of them could be completely wrong, too! Doing this isn't always easy, but it's consistent with God's commandment to honor the presence of His image in myself and others.

If we honor someone, we should assume that their inquiry about our lives is authentic. If it's an innocent, ignorant inquiry, don't be troubled by it. If it's an ignorant statement intended to offend you, don't take the bait.

If someone's words are a symbol of fear, stay calm. If they're a sign of ignorance, educate—not only with information but with your honorable demeanor. Don't assume every hurtful word is meant to hurt you. Often the person is operating out of ignorance or doesn't have the right vocabulary to express what he or she really means.

Honor your own ability to teach by responding with a question—not to start an argument but to help others hear themselves. "Are you joking around, or do you really think all Latinos are into mariachi?" By asking a question, you're giving them an opportunity to clarify what they mean.

In some cases, people need to know how they sound before they realize how offensive their words may be. Remember, most people surround themselves with like-minded people, and their views are rarely challenged. You may be the golden opportunity God has given them to rethink their perspectives.

Key #5: *Practice by just having a conversation.*
The best way to have a conversation about race . . . is to have a conversation.

Pretty deep, right? One of the main problems with communication is we simply don't practice it enough. But let me caution you against engaging in a deep conversation about racial differences with someone you don't have a relationship with. Why? Because it's just difficult. Difficult conversations are called difficult for a reason. They're difficult.

"Hi, I'm Joe. Why do you resent Arabs?"

"Hey, I'm Lisa. What do you have against Mexicans?"

Imagine how enlightening that conversation will be. Instead, first make an effort to connect around shared interests, like Jeremy did in the story he told me.

Jeremy is a salt-of-the-earth White guy from Iowa. His hometown of two thousand people included ten people of color. When he arrived in San Diego, it was culture shock to see the United Nations walking around every day.

Needless to say, Jeremy had very little experience talking with people who looked different. His main source of knowledge about people of color was the television show *Yo! MTV Raps.*

Every morning Jeremy would stop at Starbucks before work, where he was regularly served by a six-foot-three, three-hundred-pound African American man named Jim. Day in and day out, few words were spoken between Jeremy and Jim.

Neither man smiled. Jeremy ordered, Jim filled the order, and both went about their business. Compared to the other people who worked at Starbucks, Jim was quieter, so Jeremy didn't engage.

Then one day something changed. Jim saw that Jeremy was wearing a shirt with the name of a local football team, and the word *Coach.* Jim asked Jeremy when spring football started. That question sparked an hour-long conversation—and a new friendship.

Day in and day out, they talked about life. They talked about kids and the lost art of playing outdoors. They discussed the irony of how different races can play sports together but not get along outside of the stadium.

Start conversations by sharing something you have in common, just as you would with anyone of your in-group. People are people, regardless of their skin color, and everyone wants to connect, feel loved, and be valued by others. By simply having the conversation, you're having a race conversation. If the topic of race itself comes up, you'll be on solid common ground.

Key #6: Set clear boundaries.

I recently spoke with a White man who manages people of various nationalities at his job. He told me his fellow managers said he was crazy to manage so many ethnicities. He said that White managers feel like they're walking on eggshells when talking with minorities. They feel as though they can't be honest when correcting employees of a different race for fear of being called racist.

As a White manager, he often found himself avoiding difficult but necessary conversations by dancing around constructive correction. This caused minority employees to distrust him, because they sensed that his communication with them was not clear or honest. When they observed him seeming more at ease with White employees, resentment and suspicion also crept in.

Managers can justify their interactions with people of different ethnicities by saying to themselves and others that they are simply avoiding potential land mines. But managing or leading from a defensive posture dishonors their ability to have honest conversations with the employees they're responsible for leading.

Often, ethnically diverse employees feel like their manager of a different ethnicity may treat them unfairly. When they witness them interacting more freely with other employees of the manager's in-group, it reinforces the belief that racism may be a factor in their strained relationships.

Even though you can never be 100 percent sure of someone's motive, you should assume that their actions are based on ignorance or fear and not hatred. When two people don't trust each other, the worst projection they make about each other will likely happen, either in reality or in their own minds.

Bob, a White Wall Street executive, was mentoring Steve, an African American, to be a partner in a Fortune 100 company. Since this was a high-pressure, fast-paced business, there was no room for walking on eggshells or tiptoeing around hard conversations pertaining to the job.

The solution was an honest conversation about communication guidelines designed to achieve what both parties wanted: success.

Bob and Steve's conversations had to be clear about the objective of their relationship. They were both clear about the manner of communication each needed to engage in. Bob committed to being consistent in adhering to those guidelines with every employee, regardless of their ethnicity. Steve committed to giving Bob the freedom to manage him just as he managed White employees. Steve committed to judging Bob's comments based on his heart and intention to help Steve. He also committed to educating Bob on the right and wrong ways to communicate, and gave Bob room to make mistakes, thus enabling them to establish a mentoring relationship based on mutual respect. They agreed to operate on the grounds of in-group bias. Throughout this process, they became close friends.

The importance of honest conversations applies to every relationship. Allow room for mistakes and be open about what those mistakes might look like. More important, learn how to work together through apology and forgiveness. Learn what acceptable boundaries for communication are, and comply with or educate each other accordingly.

Key #7: Start in familiar environments.

Because our church is so diverse, there are opportunities for everyone to have conversations and encounters with people they would rarely, if ever, talk to outside of the church.

This was clearly illustrated in a comment made by a former corporate leader who's a member of our church. He confided that, in the confines of our building, he feels comfortable saying hi, striking up conversations, grieving with people, and hugging those he'd usually avoid being in contact with outside of the church.

He believes that, while attending church, individuals, no matter what they look like, have Christ in common and therefore feel safe with each other. But if he encountered someone who looked different from him outside the church, he confessed that his belief wouldn't be the same.

When having conversations with people outside of your normal circles, it's best to start in comfortable places where common ground exists. Take advantage of what you have in common—things you both may be learning, experiencing, or struggling with.

Before each sermon, I ask our congregation to greet someone who does not look like them. Each week I give them a new greeting to share: *God loves you, I love you, God wants to bless you today,* etc. This is designed to help them practice having race conversations. For some, these are groundbreaking interactions that serve as foundations for fruitful exchanges and relationships outside of the church.

Many White people have also told me one of the biggest reasons they're afraid to talk to people of color is their fear of offending them. Many Whites are unaware of cultural "tripwires" that may cause them to offend miniorities.

It's easier, in their minds, to keep Black friends and coworkers at arm's length rather than risk crossing a line, or coming across as racist. I realize that fear of being perceived as a racist is a big deal, and understandably so.

If you are a person of color, let me encourage you to be proactive in helping our White brothers and sisters maneuver these conversations. If you're the one who's at risk of being offended, help lower barriers to necessary race conversations by showing lots of grace to those who unintentionally catch themselves on a tripwire. And if you're the party that's scared of being called a racist, take a bold step of faith, in humility, by making an effort to engage in meaningful conversations with those of another race in spite of your fear. If both parties agree to engage in a conversation with honoring intentions, dialogue can proceed and healing will occur.

Next Steps

1. Listen to and take notes of your unfiltered thoughts about race, and consider who your internal conversations would offend if spoken aloud. Ask God to change your internal dialogue into one that honors others.

2. Practice saying *Hello, Thank you,* and *How can I serve you?* to as many people of other colors as you can. Do it until you mean it, and it starts to feel like second nature.

3. Identify someone of a different ethnicity with whom you can initiate a dialogue on race, and engage them with an honoring heart.

Prayer

"Out of the abundance of the heart the mouth speaks. A good man out of the good treasure of his heart brings forth good things, and an evil man out of the evil treasure brings forth evil things." (Matthew 12:34–35)

Lord, I know that my words come from the overflow of my heart. Please purify my thoughts about others by first challenging me in my own thought patterns. Break my habit of recurring thoughts that dishonor others. Teach me to honor others in our conversations, by speaking honest, life-giving words to them. Give me the courage, Lord, to talk with people I might normally avoid. And finally, give me the grace to allow others to say the wrong thing without taking personal offense as they grow in their ability to have difficult conversations about race.

In Jesus' powerful name, Amen.

PART IV

WE

Once we're on the same page, we can work together and enjoy each other in ways we never thought were possible. This is the ultimate goal of the Third Option: that honor would lead to joyful, Godly unity.

Demonstrating the shift of honor in relationships takes humility, patience, and a lot of work. But when it happens, it's beautiful.

CHAPTER 15

Segregated Sundays

If heaven is ethnically diverse, why aren't our churches?

In preparation for speaking at a recent citywide church event, I knew I needed to introduce myself to the local church community.

The event was in a city I'd never been to before, so I decided to visit several churches and challenge each congregation to bring their friends to the stadium. The goal of the event was to reach an ethnic cross section of the city, so I spoke at three churches in one day: an African American Church, a predominantly White church, and a Hispanic church, where I spoke in Spanish. (I've been learning Spanish for the specific purpose of connecting with the Latino community, since our church in San Diego is more than 20 percent Latino.)

The reason I had to speak in three different churches in order to reach a diverse audience is because, in America, Sunday morning is the most segregated time of the week. Eighty-seven percent of church services in America are made up of over 80 percent of one ethnicity. Generally speaking, Whites go to church with other Whites, African Americans go to church with other African Americans, and the same is true for Asians and Hispanics as well.

I believe with all my heart that the best way to fulfill God's commandments—to love Him, and to love our neighbors—is to worship Him *together*. We honor the power of God's love, which has no out-group, by allowing it to break through man-made barriers that stand between us.

I'm proposing a solution to the racial divide that you can act on as soon as you put this book down. This solution will empower the church to take a lead in fostering unity, and it all boils down to four simple words:

Count. Walk. Ask. Love.

Before we dive into what these words mean, let's take a small step back and clarify what the church's purpose really is.

Church Growth 101

I had just finished speaking at a conference in Palm Springs and was having lunch with seven other pastors when one of them asked me to help him grow his church from 1,500 to 4,000 people.

I immediately asked him, "Why?"

"Why what?"

"Why do you want to grow your church to four thousand people?"

All I heard in response was crickets.

There are many reasons why pastors might want to grow a church. They range from wanting to reach more people, to pride and competition with other churches and pastors. I was curious as to what his real motive was, and I believe he was, too. I never got an answer to my question. And if we ever crossed paths again, I'd ask him the following question: *If you do not know what you would do with four thousand people, why should God give them to you?*

To me, the *why* underlying any pastor's desire to grow a church is simple: we are called to demonstrate the love of God toward our Creator and each other. And one of the most striking ways love can be demonstrated is when the one you love doesn't look like you.

Church Mixer

When those with obvious cultural or racial differences gather in unity and love, it can seem like a modern-day miracle. Because in most congregations across our country, the reality of worshipping in a truly diverse environment is not as common.

Don't get me wrong: there's nothing wrong with a church made up of one race or culture. Being all the same does not diminish the love that church members have for each other. Besides, there are some communities that are made up of only one ethnic group. But we should consider Jesus' profound statements about friends, neighbors, and enemies when we have real options as to who we "do church" with.

> "You have heard that it was said, 'You shall love your neighbor and hate your enemy.' But I say to you, love your enemies, bless those who curse you, do good to those who hate you, and pray for those who spitefully use you and persecute you, that you may be sons of your Father in heaven..." (Matthew 5:43–45)

If that wasn't heavy enough, He goes on to ask, "If you greet your brethren only, what do you do more than others? Do not even the tax collectors do so? Therefore you shall be perfect, just as your Father in heaven is perfect" (Matthew 5:47–48).

Here's my New York translation of these verses: If you only hang out at church with folks who look and act like you, why should God be impressed?

A community that has chosen the Third Option is evident when people who've been separated are united, and when those who were fighting are now friends. When people who have very little in common allow the love of God to overcome their differences, it proves that love and honor can become the most powerful common denominators in our lives.

If there's one place on earth where this type of unity should occur, it's in and through the church. But since we have work to do in this area, let's take a closer look at why churches are segregated in the first place.

Race, Culture, and the Church

Different cultures have different tastes in music and preaching styles. Churches also often reflect the personalities and cultures of their pastors. But there's something else that speaks to the heart of why we worship with those who look like us.

For the most part, Latino, White, Black, and Asian churches address issues important to Latino, White, Black, or Asian congregants.

If you go back to the origin of the "Black church" during slavery, it was a place for Blacks to receive encouragement and hope, and address the issues pertaining to their very survival. This explains why White slave owners opposed the formation of Black churches; they feared that the unity among slaves would threaten their control.

Historian Robert R. Mathisen notes that, "Religion offered a means of catharsis, and black people retained their faith in God and found refuge in their churches. However, white society was not always willing to accept the involvement of slaves in Christianity. As one slave recounted, 'The white folks would come in when the colored people would have a prayer meeting, and whip every one of them. Most of them thought that when colored people were praying it was against them.' Organized politically and spiritually, Black churches were not only given to the teachings of Christianity but they were faithfully relied upon to address the specific issues that affected their members."[27]

Our segregated Sabbaths makes perfect sense in light of our nation's history. But as believers we're commanded to forgive the past and move toward one another in unity. The onus is on each and every believer to make a move toward each other in brotherly, honoring love. That is the very essence of the Third Option.

Today, people of all races work together, attend sporting events together, and go to school together. Nevertheless, we still worship the same God *separately*. So, even though we live in an era that appears to be more united than ever, we're still just as divided, particularly on Sunday mornings, as we were two hundred years ago. This reality breaks God's heart.

The Mission Across the Street

In an effort to foster racial unity among pastors in San Diego, I recently called a prayer meeting and invited pastors and ministry leaders from all over the county to participate.

More than 120 African-American, Asian, Latino, and White pastors and religious nonprofit leaders attended. In an attempt to encourage unity, I asked Pastor Terry Wayne Brooks of Bayview Baptist Church, a church located in a very diverse neighborhood of San Diego, to host the event.

I asked everyone to sit at a table with people they didn't know, and who didn't look like them, to exchange prayer requests and spark new relationships.

The people appreciated the diversity of those who led various parts of the meeting, and they appreciated the richness of the prayer time.

By all accounts, it seemed very productive in fostering unity, but one comment I heard during the meeting stuck with me. I heard several people say they'd never been to that part of San Diego before. And this community is literally five minutes from the heart of downtown.

American missionaries spend millions of dollars to minister to people in other countries who suffer from disease and poverty, yet many of them never think to serve those living ten minutes across town who are disenfranchised, hungry, and poor. This goes to show that some people tend to minister around their fears and biases rather than addressing them in their own backyard.

How honoring would it be for pastors to simply drive across town and learn about the challenges other pastors in their city have addressed for decades? Focusing on burdens that unite us rather than racial barriers that divide us would be a powerful step toward bridging the racial divide in the Body of Christ.

How many Black churches fail to reach out to local Hispanic churches? Hispanic churches to local Asian churches? Asian churches to White churches? The truth is, most of us in the church are guilty of ignoring the needs of those who don't look like us. But how much greater would our unity be if we acknowledged, loved, and served them instead?

We Can All Relate to Pain

Whether you live in a rich, poor, or middle-class neighborhood, on a spiritual level, the people in your town are in critical condition. Our world is sick, hurt, and dying.

Jesus addressed this pain head on:

> "The Spirit of the Lord is upon Me,
> Because He has anointed Me
> To preach the gospel to the poor;
> He has sent Me to heal the brokenhearted,
> To proclaim liberty to the captives
> And recovery of sight to the blind,
> To set at liberty those who are oppressed;
> To proclaim the acceptable year of the Lord." (Luke 4:18–19)

That's exactly what Jesus did. Then He told us to go and do the same in His name.

People all around are suffering, and the church's responsibility is to help. You might want to ask yourself, *If my church closed tomorrow, would anyone outside of my church even notice? Would anyone even care?*

God forbid our churches would close and people outside of it say, *We didn't even know it was there.*

No matter how ashamed, scared, awkward, or unprepared we might feel, we are called to love *everyone, equally.* We're not called to help and love only those we feel comfortable associating with. We're called to serve all.

Invisible Church Walls

Is it possible that unrecognized and unwanted biases and fears of pastors, church leaders, and congregations are actually preventing the church from having the impact it was designed to have? Could there be people in your community who aren't receiving the help they need because life-giving resources are sitting in the hands of those who are biased against them?

People within a few miles of your church are crying out to God for help. If you can't respond to them, due to biases or fears in your heart, God wants to work on you until that is no longer the case.

How do we make this breakthrough, you might ask? By following four simple steps that define our church's outreach philosophy.

1. Count.

It might be eye-opening to take a quantitative assessment of the pain in your surrounding community.

I'm a numbers fanatic and studied engineering in college. I can entertain myself by doing math, and I'm fully convinced you can't measure anything without a number.

In Luke 17:11–19, Jesus healed ten lepers, but only one returned to say thank you. Jesus even asked the one who returned where the other nine were. Jesus knew the numbers.

I wonder how many pastors or believers even know how many "lepers" are in your city. Of course, I don't mean literal lepers, but what about those who've been raped, molested, robbed, are addicted, or incarcerated, or those who are poor and hungry?

There are 11 abortion clinics, 17 adult bookstores, 32 drug treatment centers, 5 homeless shelters, 12 battered-women resource centers, 457 Alcoholics Anonymous meetings, 315 bars and nightclubs, 49 escort services, 17 Starbucks shops, and 16 hospitals within a ten-mile radius of our church.

Within that radius there have also been 26 murders, 337 rapes, 919 armed robberies, 9,789 thefts, and 2,991 motor vehicle thefts in the past year alone.

Why is this important for my church to know? Because it's a way to begin measuring the pain in our community. Each one of these numbers represents a person, or a multitude of people, and each one represents a family and a network of friends who suffer along with them. I wonder how much more effective we'd be in meeting the needs of our surrounding communities if we simply did a better job of accounting for them.

If you're interested in learning more about your community, you can do so immediately by visiting http://dosomethingchurch.org. Serving others is easier when we know what they suffer from and who they are. We can start by honoring those in our communities by simply caring enough to learn of their existence.

2. Walk.

Our church has over one hundred ministries led by volunteers, and each one addresses a different problem in our community.

One of our ministries is "JC's Girls," aka "Jesus Christ's Girls." These women go into strip clubs to talk to and befriend the women who work there.

JC's Girls go the extra mile for these women by supporting them in personal ways. If one of the women ends up in a child custody battle, a JC's Girl will accompany her to the courthouse. If another lands in the hospital, a JC's Girl shows up with flowers to keep her company. JC's Girls commit to walking through life with these women, offering God's unconditional love in a place and to a group of women most would consider off-limits for the church.

You and I might pass by a strip club, rehab center, or jail on our way to church and think, *Oh, I'll pray for them.* But we need to actually walk into those places and be with the people in there who are hurting. You can pray for homeless people, but that doesn't feed them. You can pray for the people in the convalescent home, but it's better to visit them. Did you know 60 percent of the people in convalescent homes have never had a visitor?

There's a world full of hurting people all around us, waiting to experience the light and love of Jesus Christ through you. Someone right now is waiting for you to come find them and share God's love. If you don't activate your purpose in their lives, they might very well die alone and without hope. Let's pledge, as a church, to never let that happen on our watch.

3. Ask.

Imagine if we stopped *telling* people what they needed to do and simply asked: *How can I help you?*

Can you imagine going to Starbucks, ordering your Frappe-lappa-chino-chica-leeky, and, after paying, asking: *And one more thing: How can I pray for you?*

Yeah, you might get some funny looks and *Uh, I'm good, thanks,* but one day you're going pick up your drink and the barista will whisper, *Hey, um, my mom has cancer, please pray for my family.*

Cancer doesn't discriminate, and offering prayer to someone who doesn't look like you is just as easy as offering it to someone who does. Let's start asking today. It's so simple, and so powerful.

But be ready for what comes next.

4. Love.

Based on decades of research, I've concluded something about women: they're complicated.

Why? Because every single woman has her own unique requirements and rules on how she wants to be loved. Don't get me wrong, men are complicated, too, but in different ways.

To make matters more interesting, these rules of love are only known by the woman. This is very mind-boggling to us men. You can see this in the conversations of teenage girls.

"He doesn't act right."

"Nope. He doesn't get it. He doesn't understand."

"Maybe I need to tell him, because he doesn't know what to say or do."

"You better *not* tell him. He's supposed to know."

I'm joking but you get the point. Love can feel complicated sometimes. But when it comes to loving God and your neighbor, the commandment is very simple and clear. Do you know how to love God? My paraphrase of what Jesus said about loving him boils down to this: *If you love Me, do what I say. Even when you don't feel like it.* (John 14:15)

Love simply means asking the question "How can I help you?" and responding to the answer you get in a manner that's consistent with honoring God.

Imagine if we measured the pain of our communities and picked one area that grabbed ahold of our hearts. I'm sure some numbers I listed above about people in pain caused compassion to stir in your soul.

What if you researched convalescent homes because you had a heart for the elderly? Or group homes because you love to mentor kids in foster care? What if you walked in and asked: *How can I help?* And then, what if you followed through with love, meeting their needs in a manner that honors God's heart for them?

Your city can be utterly transformed by these simple acts of obedience on your part: count, walk, ask, love. Your heart, in turn, will be transformed by obeying God's commandment to love your neighbors, turning the whole situation into a win-win for the church and the world.

Is there a community in your city you haven't visited? One that you fear or feel uncomfortable going to?

Is there a community that God has called you to help but you've said no?

Is there a situation of pain in a certain demographic that you know exists, but you haven't taken the time to research or assess?

Have you found yourself hesitating to offer God's love to others because you're afraid of being rejected?

If you answered yes to any of these questions, it might be time to commit to counting, walking, asking, and loving.

Next Steps

1. Partner with someone who looks different from you, and apply the "count, walk, ask, love" model to people you meet together.

It could be at your local coffee shop, a convalescent home, a school where kids need after-school tutoring, or on the street—wherever the greatest needs in your community are. Simply walk up to them and ask, "How can we help?"

2. Try visiting a church where the congregants look nothing like you. See how it feels being the "other" one Sunday morning, and allow God to develop new friendships with those you meet. Experience the presence of God in a different environment.

3. If you're a pastor, consider partnering with two or three pastors from different neighborhoods in your city to address a common cause together. If more churches partnered in pursuit of a common goal, barriers to segregated Sundays could one day disappear for good.

Prayer

"When the Son of Man comes in His glory, and all the holy angels with Him, then He will sit on the throne of His glory. All the nations will be gathered before Him, and He will separate them one from another, as a shepherd divides his sheep from the goats." (Matthew 25:31–32)

If heaven is diverse, our churches should be too. Churches that look like the kingdom are best equipped to represent the kingdom to the world.

Dear Lord, I ask that You stir my heart to serve people who look different from me. I ask that You stir the hearts of church leaders in my city to desire friendship and partnership with those who are from different backgrounds. May we, as the church, tackle the challenges in our own cities together, as one family.

In Your name I pray, Amen.

CHAPTER 16

———————

My Brother's and Sister's Keeper

Is there some resentment in your heart?

"My brother, how are you dealing with your issue with White people?" I asked.

He chuckled and walked away.

The next time I saw him, I asked, "My brother, have you heard of internalized racism?"

"No. What's that?"

Five days later: "My brother, do you know what in-group bias is?"

"Never heard of it."

A week later: "Dude, have you heard of unconscious bias?"

"I think so."

Over the past year, as I slowly acquainted myself with these terms, I'd share them with Darrel, an African American friend of mine. It was an ongoing dialogue between us. Every time I saw him I'd hit him with a new phrase, and every week he responded the same way: "I never heard of that. Where are you getting all of this information?"

This went on every week until he started tracking me down for the word or phrase of the week. We began discussing the meaning of these terms and the degree to which we've experienced them. We shared examples of how we and others have experienced various forms of racism and how those experiences have affected us.

Over several months I noticed a change in Darrel's eyes. He showed increased interest and conviction in learning these phrases, which attached a name to the feelings he'd experienced throughout his life. I could tell certain topics hit him harder than others, because he'd stare off into space as examples of the issues we discussed raced through his mind.

Eventually, I started asking him about his own biases. "How are you doing with all this? Do you have some racism to deal with in your own life? Is there some resentment in your heart?" At first he'd just chuckle and walk away. But one day he admitted to me that he needed to forgive some people—specifically some White people! This came to the surface when I told him about unforgiveness's ugly children.

When you harbor an unforgiving spirit toward someone or to a group of people, over time it bears some pretty heinous children: resentment, retaliation, jealousy, anger, and bitterness, to name a few. When I shared this with him, it was as though all these "children" started throwing a tantrum at once, fearing they would be kicked out of his heart.

These conversations turned into an opportunity to challenge Darrel about his own biases, and he often asked me if I thought he was a racist. I then asked, "What do *you* think?" As time went on, as his anger and hurt became obvious, I'd confront him by saying, "You have some issues, brother." We discussed how he couldn't justify being racist just because he was angry and hurt at those who'd been racist toward him throughout his life.

Eventually he admitted that he was bitter toward certain individuals. His family and friends had had many bad experiences with White people, which caused resentment and bitterness to grow. Our conversations helped him realize just how often he made race-based comments that were negative and destructive to himself and to others.

In calling him out—in truth and with love—I was acting as my brother's keeper.

A "Keeper"

If we're going to develop a culture of mutual honor, it will require God's people to lovingly hold each other accountable. That's what I mean by being each other's "keeper."

After Cain killed his brother Abel, which was the very first recorded murder in the Bible, God confronted him and asked where his brother was. Cain responded by saying, "I do not know. Am I my brother's keeper?" (Genesis 4:9). In other words, Cain was asking, "Am I responsible for my brother's well-being?"

The answer is *yes*.

We are created to live in a relationship of honor and healthy accountability with one another. When we're in accountable relationships, we're less likely to be dishonoring to others. We have a responsibility to hold our brothers and sisters to a high standard of honor, and to be held to the same standard by them as well. The way we do this for each other is by "speaking the truth in love" (Ephesians 4:15). When we see something, we must call it out—at the right time, and with the right attitude of loving correction.

Both of my grandmothers grew up in Jamaica, West Indies, but it was my dad's mom who loved to garden. She was so used to being surrounded by plants that when she moved to Queens, New York, she kept at least one hundred plants growing in her basement, in addition to her garden outside.

On every visit to her house, we spent time "keeping" her plants by watering, pruning, and fertilizing them. To "keep" plants means to guard, protect, and nurture an environment where they may grow and flourish. My grandmother planted the garden knowing the potential for beautiful flowers and bouquets. She nurtured the plants because each had the potential to develop its own flowers. If we didn't do our part to prune and nurture them, we'd limit their potential and jeopardize their growth.

A brother's or a sister's keeper is someone who nurtures growth in another person. It isn't a watchdog relationship, where you're keeping an eye on them, but rather a shepherding relationship—a protective one in the context of mutual accountability. You must have a heart for another person's growth and well-being. You must have a passion to help them *do* right rather than a desire to *be* right.

Being a brother's or sister's keeper is humbly recognizing that we all have blind spots that require another's perspective to identify in our own lives. It takes a lot of humility to admit you've struggled with various forms of dishonor, but doing so is a prerequisite to offering advice to others.

At times, while in the presence of White people, I've heard them make negative statements that reinforce false stereotypes about minorities. Generally they're comments that weren't meant for my ears. But I often wonder: *What would they say if they knew I'd overheard them?*

This issue is far from being unique to White people. In fact, people in every self-identified in-group talk trash about people in their out-group. This includes Asians, Latinos, Blacks, women, men, children, parents—you name it. And the only accountability they have is that of their keepers. Keepers are precious and important, and we should all seek to surround ourselves with them, because they and only they can be trusted to rebuke and correct us when we need to readjust our thinking toward God-honoring thoughts, words, actions, and deeds.

We all know who the hard-core racists or angry people in *our* cultures are. That's where we potentially come in. They just *might* listen to someone who's like them. A friend. A keeper.

We "keep" our brothers or sisters—and anyone else over whom we have influence—by reminding them of their calling to love their neighbors, and challenging them to think and act honorably toward them. Our brothers and sisters make up the concentric circles of our relationships. They are family, friends, coworkers, and anyone with whom we have influence. At times, even strangers can fall into this category.

Our influence has the potential to reach far beyond our inner circle, and can impact entire communities with the challenge to become more honorable. The first and potentially most powerful "keeper" relationship we're responsible for is the relationship we have with the impressionable children in our lives.

MJ and MC

A majority of my California-based family is light-skinned Black, and my grandson is no exception. He looks just like his dad, my son, who's very light-skinned. This is why we call him "Lemonade"—a term of endearment in our family.

Because two-year-olds have a very small circle of people they spend their time with, my grandson is mainly with light-skinned people. At the age of two he met my best friend from high school, who is considerably darker than my family. In addition, my friend is still rocking the Afro we all had in high school a long, long time ago.

It just so happened that when my friend was visiting, I was babysitting my grandson. So my grandson and I spent the better part of two days with my friend and his Afro. My grandson's nickname is MJ, and my friend from high school's nickname is MC. Needless to say, they bonded really well. For two days, all I heard was "MC!" "MJ!" "MC!" "MJ!"

After MC went home, my grandson looked for him everywhere, asking for MC by name, and wanting to FaceTime with him. And ever since that day, every time he sees another dark-skinned brother with an Afro he yells, "That's MC!"

Then he looks at me and asks, "MC's your friend?"

"He's my *best* friend," I answer.

Then he repeats, "MC's your *best* friend."

Aside from the fact that I wanted my grandson and my best friend to hang out, the opportunity to nurture a sense of honor and respect in my grandson for those who look like MC wasn't lost on me.

It's one thing to see people every now and then, but entirely different to spend an extended period of time with them developing a relationship. Those few days we spent hanging out with MC sent a message to my grandson that anybody with a dark complexion and an Afro could be Grampy's best friend—not someone to fear but someone to befriend.

Your Children's Keeper

What message are you sending your children about the types of people who are friendly, important, safe, smart, or valuable? And what message are you sending them about the types of people who are unfriendly, unimportant, unsafe, ignorant, or invaluable?

Desegregation of the military, schools, restaurants, hotels, and neighborhoods occurred in the 1960s, but for some, segregation is still a reality in America today. Many people today self-segregate to "protect" their kids from the influence of certain out-groups. They do this by raising them in carefully chosen neighborhoods, sending them to certain schools, and developing relationships with only those they want their kids to be influenced by.

These well-meaning parents are, intentionally or unintentionally, sending a message to their children that certain groups of people shouldn't be valued the way others should be. And naturally children pick up on the cues their parents send, internalizing these beliefs for themselves.

Some people speak in code about "good schools" and "good neighborhoods." What they might actually mean is that good schools and good neighborhoods are those that exclude certain people. That is, in essence, what makes them "good" in their minds.

When I asked those who embarked on my field trip experiment why they were scared of certain ethnic groups they'd never been personally threatened by, all of them had to think long and hard before answering. Some of them identified the genesis of their fear in what they picked up from others in their childhood—a relic of the past that they'd carried into adulthood.

Children are like sponges: they soak up whatever's in their environment. That's true whether the environment is positive or negative. So when parents intentionally act to include or exclude certain groups of people from their social circles, children take note of their parents' actions and internalize the belief systems that are modeled for them. This can have long-lasting effects that reach into adulthood—effects that are either positive or negative, depending on how their parents raised them.

Take a look at the types of people your kids interact with and are surrounded by. Parents who socialize their children by exposing them to many cultures enable their kids to relate to a wider range of people. They also set a precedent for how their children will treat and interact with those who represent different ethnicities and cultures. These relationships, or lack thereof, will have an impact on the types of people your children are learning to be the most comfortable with. They will also influence who your children learn to be the most uncomfortable with.

To be a keeper for your children, nieces, nephews, and grandchildren, it's important to nurture God-honoring experiences and relationships and intentionally provide a well-rounded perspective and understanding of people representing all races. Seek opportunities for you and your children to build relationships with people of all backgrounds whether they're from the other side of the tracks or the other side of the world. Some of these relationships may be new to you, but I urge you to use them as growth opportunities to step beyond your comfort zone for the benefit of your children.

Intentional Relationships

Whenever football lovers think of the NFL's Dallas Cowboys, they also think of the team's owner, Jerry Jones. But the person we *should* know about is Charlotte Jones Anderson, his daughter. Charlotte is the Dallas Cowboys' executive vice president and chief brand officer and, in the opinion of many, the most powerful woman in the NFL.

You might imagine Charlotte grew up with a silver spoon, and she did. But Charlotte made a decision when she was a sophomore in high school to voluntarily leave her mostly White private school and attend Little Rock Central High School. This public school was made famous in 1957 when Arkansas governor Orval Faubus blocked nine African American students from attending what had been a segregated campus. It took President Dwight Eisenhower and the National Guard to integrate the school.

When Charlotte enrolled in Little Rock Central High School, the student population was more than 60 percent Black. Charlotte intentionally chose to become the "other." She was the captain of her 75 percent Black cheerleading squad and ran for student body president against a popular Black football player.

"I needed to try something different," she said. "I just felt like the environment I was in was so sheltered and so very insular that there had to be more. I believed that in order to really understand people, you had to go and be with people."[34]

If Charlotte, as a fifteen-year-old, had the courage to leave her comfort zone for a new high school where she was the "other," we can surely find the courage to invite a coworker of a different ethnicity to lunch. It could be the start of one of the greatest friendships of your life.

The younger a child is when they develop relationships with people of different ethnicities, the less likely they will be to grow up with negative biases and racist perspectives toward others. Do your children—and yourself—a favor: start the process of socializing them with people of other ethnicities today.

Workplace Keepers

At the end of each year, partners in a particular law firm met with each of their associates to talk about adjustments in base compensation, bonuses, and professional development.

Ralph, an African American partner, led these meetings, along with two White partners. Bobby, a young White associate, was the first to meet with them. One of the White partners opened by saying, "We looked at your performance last year, and this is what we recommend for your new base salary and year-end bonus."

Bobby shot back, "You know what, I really appreciate that proposal, but that's unacceptable to me. You missed a few things, and I think you need to reconsider these cases, then come back with another proposal."

After Bobby left the room, one of the White partners said, "He's just the kind of guy we need in this firm. He knows what he's worth, he's confident, and he's sure of his work. Let's reconsider what we've offered."

The next attorney to be interviewed was LuLu, a Black female associate of the firm. After hearing their review and offer, she said, "It seems you haven't considered all my accomplishments last year, and I'd like you to take a look at my work and reconsider your offer."

After she left the room, one White partner said, "Wow, she's really angry. We put a good-faith proposal on the table. She doesn't appreciate what we've offered her or the opportunity she has with this firm. Maybe we need to tell her that if she doesn't like our proposal, she should come up with some new numbers or look elsewhere."

Ralph spoke up and said, "We just talked to Bobby. He pushed back, and we were all proud of him for doing it. But when LuLu pushed back and used almost the same words as Bobby, you perceived her as being angry. Furthermore, before she even walked in the room, you were braced for a fight: you said, 'Here comes Lulu. This is going to be really tense.'"

According to Ralph, many minority lawyers end up moving to different firms in their third or fourth year because they didn't have anyone holding partners accountable behind closed doors. In this case, the White partners recognized their double standard and reconsidered their offer. Ralph provided real value to the firm by being his partners' keeper.

We must be willing to stand up for people who can't stand up for themselves. We must use our privilege and influence to ensure that everyone is treated honorably. The best and most honoring way to do this is by becoming your brother's and sister's keeper, helping people recognize and respond positively to a blind spot they can't see in themselves.

The Stuttering Manager

Laura, a White woman, was both an employee at a local San Diego Christian school and the "school mom" where her two kids attended.

While shopping for groceries down the hill from her home, she noticed a part-time job in her local grocery store. When she drove home, she told "T," a student who was temporarily living with her family, about the opportunity. He immediately went to the store to apply for the job but returned home in ten minutes, his head hanging in defeat.

"Why are you back so soon?" Laura asked. "Did you get the job?"

He replied "No, they said they're not hiring."

Before the rest of the story was out of his mouth, she grabbed her keys and drove down to the store.

When she got there, she found the manager and said, "Excuse me sir, but are you hiring? I saw your sign that says that you have part-time jobs available."

He replied, "Absolutely we are hiring."

She said, "Hmm, that's odd, because my son just came here and was told that you said you weren't hiring." Even though T wasn't her biological son, she loved him as if he were.

"No, ma'am, we have part-time jobs available."

"So, is it that you're only hiring White people and not Black people? If that's the case, you need to write on the sign that Black people need not apply." At this point a crowd had gathered around Laura's verbal beatdown of the now-stuttering manager.

T is short for Tyrone, the Black student who temporarily lived with Laura and her family. Even after Laura rushed to his defense, T never went back to that store. The damage had been done, and he would remember that scarring incident for the rest of his life. He will, however, remember Laura's love even more.

Laura, however, was a true brother's keeper. She was willing to confront someone who was "like her"—another White person—to support someone who was not like her: a Black kid named Tyrone.

Also, notice how she referred to him as her "son." While he lived with her, she loved Tyrone like he was a member of her family. When you are in the position to act as a brother's or sister's keeper, the first thing you might do is ask yourself what name you are using to refer to the person who is being mistreated. If you have given them a dishonoring label, it will be that much easier to tolerate them being dishonored. If, however, you honor them by calling them a friend or a family member, you're far more likely to honor them in your heart and stand up for them when they are mistreated.

Laura's story proves that we all have far more influence than we realize. What we say about people, how we treat them, the time and nature of the attention we give to them, and pretty much everything we do toward them can impact the way others treat them as well.

To underscore this point, our children, friends, family, and coworkers constantly take cues from our reactions to their comments and actions toward people we'd categorize as "others." If we react negatively to their dishonoring statements and actions, it will send a signal to them that what they said was inappropriate, and hopefully cause their behavior to cease. If we don't react or, worse, play along, it will signal that we approve of their inappropriate comments, and they will continue to act inappropriately.

We get to choose what kind of world we want to live in and what kind of world the next generation will live in. And with our actions and words, we have an opportunity to influence it every day.

Next Steps

1. Commit to being your brother's or sister's keeper for at least one person in your life. Once you decide who that will be, write their name here: _____.

2. Identify one specific way you can act as a keeper to that person. Try to identify one attitude or behavior that you know that they need to be challenged in, and ask God to help you reveal that to them with tact, love, and honor.

3. Instead of getting angry or defensive, use one of these lines this
   week to challenge someone who says something that comes
   across as racially derogatory:

> *What do you mean by that?*
>
> *Do you really believe that?*
>
> *Have you had firsthand experience about that subject?*
>
> *Has anyone actually treated you that way?*
>
> *I don't think that's funny.*
>
> *Would you be offended if someone said that about you?*
>
> *Do you personally know that person or anyone like them?*

Prayer

As iron sharpens iron, so a man sharpens the countenance of his friend.
(Proverbs 27:17)

*Dear God, I realize I can't truly learn to be honorable without a brother's
or sister's keeper. And I accept the challenge to be another's keeper. Please
help me speak up against dishonor, and be an example of honor in my own
life. Give me the courage to challenge someone else to live more honorably.
Give me a loving and patient heart to express correction, and prepare the
hearts of those to whom I speak to receive correction with humility. I ask
for you to "keep" me, by sending someone into my life to hold me accountable for my words and actions.*

In Your loving name I pray, Amen.

CHAPTER 17

Culture Wars

What people do and how they do it . . .

A while back, I was walking through the Dallas airport with a friend of mine, and he noticed I was saying hello to random African American guys as they walked by.

If we made eye contact, I'd say something like "What's up?" or simply nod to acknowledge them. After witnessing this for several minutes, my friend, who is White, asked, "Do you know all those guys?"

"No, most Black guys do that to each other."

He laughed in disbelief and said, "No way!"

"Watch this," I told him. The next time I made eye contact with another brother, I nodded and said, "What's up?" He responded likewise.

My friend was stunned. Then I asked him, "Why don't you try that with one of *your* people?"

He laughed and said, "I don't think so!"

We came from, and belonged to, different cultures. When Black men acknowledge each other, it's a way of saying, *Wazup? I see you, you good? I got you!* It's what we do. But he'd never noticed it before, because it's not part of his culture.

What Is Culture?

Culture is simply *what people do and how they do it.*

In the context of this book, culture is the way ethnic groups generally do things based on what people care about the most. The universal concerns we all share—life, liberty, and the pursuit of happiness—can be expressed in many unique ways.

We all care about developing meaningful, loving, and compatible relationships. We all care about having healthy families and raising children who succeed in life. And the ways families are developed varies in different cultures, but they aren't as different as they might first appear.

We all have the desire to fulfill our purposes in life, and want to freely pursue our hopes and dreams. We all have our own way of communicating with one another, not only in the form of a spoken language, but also in the form of unspoken mannerisms.

We desire to express all our uniqueness and creativity. We all need to give and receive love. And precisely how that love is expressed in our groups reflects the beautiful imagination of our Creator.

So culture can definitely unite us. But culture, as we know, more often creates division.

Cultural Divides

Out of our pride, we often think that *our* culture, or the way our ethnic group pursues universal desires, is best. Consequently, we tend to discount or marginalize how other cultures operate. When this happens, culture becomes a dividing line and a reason to avoid those who aren't like us.

Instead of letting them become fodder for bias, I believe that cultural differences can be used to feed growth and unity. Instead of allowing our differences to divide us, I believe we can honor one another by choosing to learn from each other.

We honor people by appreciating the creative ways they've chosen to follow their dreams, prepare meals, raise their kids, dress, communicate, and support each other. We embrace cultural differences by establishing common goals and observing how others reach them in their own unique ways. By doing so, we'll develop more meaningful relationships, grounded in sincere appreciation, curiosity, and, eventually, a better understanding of each other's culture.

Million-Dollar Questions

Before we go deep into the topic of culture, I need to ask three million-dollar questions. My questions won't cost a million dollars, but they will give you insight that's worth a million dollars.

Million-dollar question #1: Do you feel as though your culture is better than every other culture?
Let me pose this question another way: Do you believe there is nothing to learn from other cultures, especially those you are biased against? If the answer is yes, then all I have to say is, *Wow! We'd all love to learn from your culture.* But if your answer is *No, I think I can learn from others,* then you're on your way to a whole new cultural adventure.

Million-dollar question #2: Are you willing to humbly look for ways to learn from other cultures, especially those you may knowingly or unknowingly have a bias against?
Pride won't allow you to learn from other people, so you'll need to posture yourself so that you're intentionally humble in this pursuit.

Here's an important cultural disclaimer: there are negative, discriminatory, and harmful cultural practices in this world, so I'm not advocating that we agree with everyone and everything. There's no need to throw your brain and values out the window in the name of cultural appreciation. That said, the opposite is often true of Americans: generally speaking, we've chosen to buy into the cultural standards we were raised with while discounting all other cultures and eliminating the opportunity for growth and discovery.

The way your culture does things is not necessarily the way you have to continue doing things. My hope is that this book will challenge you to live differently today, without first waiting for the culture around you to change.

Million-dollar question #3: How do we distinguish a good cultural practice from a bad one?

Steve, a Mexican kid, was serving time in the juvenile jail. While playing basketball on the yard, the ball rolled out of bounds and bumped into an African American kid.

"Sorry, man," Steve said as he retrieved the ball.

Within five seconds he was surrounded by other Mexican kids who screamed, "We *never* apologize to a N*!" Prison culture groomed Steve to never again honor a Black person—a cultural trait he carried with him out of prison, until . . . well, more on that later.

Sometimes, culture actually dictates bias.

Just as culture dictates the way we do things, it also dictates the way we *don't* do things. We must recognize that there may be an aspect of our culture that's hindering our growth and ability to honor those who are different.

You know your culture is hurting you when "the way you do things" hinders you from honoring the humanity of others. Ask yourself: *Does the way I do things prevent me from learning from a rich Asian person? From a poor White person? From a middle-class Black person? From a working-class Latino? Or from anyone else who doesn't act or look like me?*

Does your culture force everyone from a certain racial out-group into one negative mold? And does your culture influence the way you view people from that racial group today?

Jesus often confronted religious leaders who chose to follow culture over the laws of God. In Matthew 15, he takes the Pharisees on about one of their man-made rules, which relegated the needs of their parents, whom God commands us to honor, as secondary to the religious practice of devoting gifts to God on the altar. Here's the exchange, in classic Jesus fashion:

> Jesus [said], "And why do you break the command of God for the sake of your tradition? For God said, 'Honor your father and mother' and 'Anyone who curses their father or mother is to be put to death.' But you say that if anyone declares that what might have been used to help their father or mother is 'devoted to God,' they are not to 'honor their father or mother' with it. Thus you nullify the word of God for the sake of your tradition. You hypocrites! Isaiah was right when he prophesied about you:
>
> "'These people honor me with their lips, but their hearts are far from me. They worship me in vain; their teachings are merely human rules.'"

Is it possible that you claim to honor God and the image He's placed in you, but, like the Pharisees in this story, you are actually honoring the culture of man?

Common Sense

Jason was a White, six-foot-three-inch traveling insurance salesman whose route covered low-income Black, Asian, and Latino communities in San Diego, Orange County, and Los Angeles.

When his coworkers heard about the neighborhoods he was assigned to canvass, they encouraged him to stay away from those areas. But he refused to heed their warnings, because the neighborhoods were in his assigned area and he felt responsible for serving those who lived there. So he proceeded to sell insurance in his assigned neighborhoods, walking door to door in communities his colleagues had advised him to avoid.

Walking his rounds, he met people of all ethnicities. Some of the homes he visited had only one English speaker, someone who spoke broken English at best. Many homes he visited had several Latino, Vietnamese, or African American guys hanging out on their front lawns or porches, drinking 40s (forty-ounce bottles of beer). He received many awkward stares from people who were surprised to see a White dude like him in their neighborhoods. The looks were understandable, and, to Jason's credit, he didn't automatically assume the worst about those who stared.

After visiting several dozen homes, Jason realized that, no matter how awkward it was at first, once he connected with folks on a human level, there was an immediate shift in their relationship. The scene went from one White guy and six Latinos, or one guy and five Vietnamese, to just a group of people talking about kids, sports, food, and aspects of life we all care about.

The tension and awkwardness were replaced with genuine friendliness. But how exactly did he break the ice?

Jason learned to look around the living room for family pictures, sporting gear, or items related to something they might have in common. We're all designed to pursue dreams, enjoy hobbies, develop talents, and work toward success. We all want to be valued, loved, and appreciated for how we pursue life, liberty, and happiness. Their pictures captured the moments each family held dear, and through them Jason could almost always find some thread of commonality between his life and theirs.

When Jason wasn't connecting as readily as he'd like, he'd ask for a glass of water. Without fail, his hosts would jump up, apologize, and bring him water. Why? Because all people want to be hospitable and welcoming. This simple gesture often led to an offer to share some food, which in all cultures is a form of love. How food is prepared and served varies from culture to culture, but its power to connect is the same.

What started out as a goal for Jason—to sell insurance—turned into a lesson on how to establish relationships with people who didn't look like him. His determination to honor and serve families outside of his comfort zone and culture gave him the ability to look every person in the eye and give them the respect they deserved.

As members of the human race, the values we share far outweigh our differences. When we choose to look for commonality with others, their lights and ours shine in recognition of each other.

> "No one, when he has lit a lamp, puts it in a secret place or under a basket, but on a lampstand, that those who come in may see the light. The lamp of the body is the eye. Therefore, when your eye is good, your whole body also is full of light. But when your eye is bad, your body also is full of darkness." (Luke 11:33–34)

If you're looking for a reason to segregate, you will find one. But if you're looking for reasons to honor and unite, you'll find many.

Goals and Values

Many people comment about Asians' uncanny ability to excel academically, but according to my friend Helen there's a lot that goes into this cultural stereotype.

Helen, who is from China, explained to me how kids in her culture were groomed not only to excel in school but to compete for the best jobs, and because there were so few good jobs in relation to the number of kids, the competition was intense. She told me that for her, it all started with the high expectations her parents set for her to get a good education and establish a successful career.

In many American families, the focus is on completing your homework before you play, but in Helen's family it was different. Since the family's objective was for Helen to earn the best grades, attend the best schools, and be hired into the best careers, just "doing your homework" wasn't good enough.

It is not uncommon in a Chinese family, Helen told me, for children to attend school all day and then be tutored until late afternoon or early evening. Most of their childhood is consumed with striving to earn exceptional grades, and it's a family endeavor. Parents play a big role in helping their children succeed.

When you have a group of people who are all striving to achieve the same goals, and when parents in the same neighborhood are pushing their kids to compete for the best schools and the best jobs, momentum is created. *The way people do things*—in other words, culture—materializes.

We tend to live up or down to the expectations placed on us by our families and culture. Does this story imply that Chinese culture is the only culture that values excelling at education? Of course not. Does it mean that this cultural practice is all good? Not necessarily. The question we must ask ourselves isn't whether the culture is good or bad but rather *What can I learn from other cultures to improve my own life?*

Personally, I wish I'd had a little more academic discipline in my life when I was young. My focus was on excelling in football so that I could make it to the pros. I had no vision for any other career, no academic goals, and no role models in business or medicine to consider emulating. I could have benefited a lot from a good dose of Helen's Chinese culture!

I refer back to one of my million-dollar questions: *Are you open to learning from other cultures?*

What does your culture value? Money? Family? God? Education? Are you satisfied with the cultural value you've placed on learning, family unity, spiritual growth, academic success, or any other areas that are important to you? What can you learn from other cultures, and adopt in your own life that would help you in the areas you'd like to excel in? We can change and grow by learning from other cultures, or by the way other families do things within our own culture.

We dishonor ourselves and our potential by selling ourselves short. Don't aspire to a standard set by anyone else that doesn't challenge you to excel. It doesn't matter what your culture embraces: the reality is, cultures can elevate us or bring us down. Take what you must from other cultures to achieve what you want. You're lucky to live in a country where there are so many cultures to learn from! Take advantage of that privilege and do what works for you.

Your Choices Shape Your Life and Your Culture

Dr. Myron Rolle is a Bahamian American, a former safety in the National Football League, a Rhodes scholar, and a neurosurgeon. In other words, he's a total slacker—*not!*

While playing ball at Florida State University, Myron was named as a finalist for a Rhodes scholarship from Oxford University. Part of the process included an in-person interview, which happened to be scheduled on the same day as a football game against Maryland.

After the interview, where he was awarded the scholarship, he took a charter flight to the University of Maryland, where his team won 37–3.

Myron was only the fourth Florida State student, and the only FSU football player, to ever receive a Rhodes scholarship. After graduation, he postponed his NFL career for a year to complete his studies at Oxford, where he received a master's degree in medical anthropology.

Pretty impressive, right? Oh, but we're just getting started!

After returning to the States, he was drafted by the Tennessee Titans in the sixth round of the 2010 NFL Draft. When his football career ended, he attended the Florida State University College of Medicine and Harvard Medical School, followed by a residency program at Massachusetts General Hospital.

"I'm glad I walked into my purpose," Rolle told an interviewer recently.[35]

I love Myron's story because it's an example of someone who shattered racial stereotypes and rejected negative cultural perceptions. It's critically important not to peg, or limit, cultural tendencies to an entire race.

Though cultural tendencies influence all people, Latinos, Whites, or Blacks shouldn't be expected to embrace all the same cultural habits as their peers. When they do, stereotypes form and limit their potential for growth as individuals.

In my own way, I fell victim to this tendency. As I've said, in high school I wasn't an academically minded athlete, even though deep inside I knew I was smarter than my grades revealed. The culture of my family and close circle of friends simply didn't value academics the way Myron does.

Myron's example of academic excellence could have radically changed the course of my life. Unfortunately, I didn't have any role models like him growing up. This is why it's important to learn from other cultures: yours may be limiting your full potential, but there are many others that could significantly influence your life and your entire culture in a positive way. Myron is an impressive example of someone who's changing the Black athlete culture for the better, and I pray that more like him will follow.

Groups and Worldview

In Chapter 2, I introduced the idea of how we all belong to, and identify ourselves as part of, an in-group that is often dictated by gender, color, or race. But in some cultures, that in-group or communal bond[36] is a worldview that impacts the way members of the group relate to others.

Black, Latino, and Asian cultures tend to identify themselves as being born into a larger family and see the world through the lens of belonging to that group. Individuality is less important than the common good.

By contrast, Northern European cultures tend to view themselves as individuals. Consequently, White Americans tend to focus more on their individual well-being than on the good of the whole. This isn't a political statement; it's just a reflection of their origins and the culture from which their value system originates.

Let me clarify that this does not mean that those who come from an individualistic mind-set do not care for others. Nor am I implying that those who come from a communal culture do not have individualistic goals and drive. I'm simply highlighting the lens through which their cultural views on life are shaped.

In the story I shared about walking through the airport, I acknowledged brothers who I identified as being part of my in-group. Even though I don't personally know them, we all are part of the same extended family. We view each other as united under similar circumstances.

When people have a worldview filtered by their group or communal orientation, they feel the pain of others in their group. When someone from *another* group offends someone from *our* group, we all take it personally. We also tend to view the offender as a representative of their entire racial group, because that is how we view the world: in groups.

This tendency to view the world in a group orientation helps explain the community-wide protests against police violence toward Black men. In the Black community, when one person kills a Black person, we all feel the pain and attribute it to an action taken by one group against another. This feeling is a natural result of our group or communal orientation.

Individuals from communally oriented societies tend to see themselves as born into a community for life. In individually oriented societies, people tend to grow up looking out for themselves, organizing their own families and friends independently, and doing what they feel they need to do in order to create the lives they want to live.

Workplace relationships, for example, have more of a family dynamic for communal cultures, while they tend to be viewed more contractually by individualistic cultures. When you view yourself as an individual first, it's natural to assume that other people see themselves as individuals as well.

Which cultural perspective is right? Neither—and both! The truth is, we are better off if we can learn from both perspectives. We'll also be better equipped to solve the issue of racism in our country when we examine the actions of "others" through the lens of their cultural orientations.

How honoring it would be if those who grew up in individually oriented cultures would spend time nurturing those whose well-being is tied to a larger group! Imagine the healing that could flow from acknowledging their value and affirming their sense of belonging—not only as an individual but as a member of a group they value!

How honoring it would be for those whose culture leans toward a communal identification to leave room for God to give them a plan for their own lives! God may have a plan that shatters the mold of anyone in their group—but they wouldn't know it until they allowed themselves to adopt a more individualistic mind-set. And how awesome would it be if the very same communally minded people could respect the need for others' individualistic tendencies? Doing so would not only honor others, but also help this group separate the actions of individuals from those of a group that doesn't identify itself as homogenous.

Adopting a posture of honor is the essence of the Third Option, which opens you up to a whole new level of understanding of the world around you. As the Scriptures proclaim, "No eye has seen or ear has heard what God has prepared for you" (1 Corinthians 2:9). Be open to the cultural shifts God may be urging you to adopt, and experience the blessings that accompany your obedience.

Sports Culture

An NFL sideline is so loud and chaotic, you can barely hear yourself, much less hear the coaches yelling at you.

Every time you come off the field, you get an earful from a coach about something. Players are constantly making adjustments and getting corrected for things they've done wrong. Guys are running on and off the field like a nonstop fire drill. Others are coming to the sidelines bleeding, coddling dislocated fingers, hobbling with sprained ankles, or wobbling off with concussions.

During one game in San Diego against the Dallas Cowboys, Mike Green, our middle linebacker and my workout partner, was escorted off the field by two of our coaches. As they moved past me, I could hear him moaning and groaning in pain. To put things into perspective, Mike was our defensive rookie of the year. He was a force in the middle of the line, taking on guys fifty pounds heavier than he was on just about every play. So when I saw him being carried off, I thought to myself, *He's not coming back anytime soon.*

Two plays later Mike was standing next to me, snapping his helmet on, and telling the coach, "I'm ready, boss." Back on the field he ran.

I remember playing with a badly sprained knee in a game against the Denver Broncos. As I caught a punt, I focused on not cutting to my left or right, to prevent my knee from buckling.

Culture refers to the way we do things, and one of the most important aspects of the NFL culture is the expectation that you will give your all for your teammates, no matter what. If you don't produce, there's someone else who's ready and waiting to take your place. The NFL is a place of intense commitment, self-sacrifice, and personal responsibility. Every team member expects you to give 110 percent of yourself in practice, meetings, the weight room, and game time.

We each brought personal beliefs and habits to the team, but we were willing to lay them aside for the greater goal of unity and winning. The NFL culture required us to make huge sacrifices for the good of the team. We all played with pain, trained past exhaustion, and denied ourselves certain pleasures that could hinder our preparation and performance. And we did it all willingly, for the greater good. Most important, if someone did not live up to that standard, he was held accountable, and it usually wasn't pretty.

Imagine if we could all adopt an aspect of the NFL's culture by honoring everyone's right to be on our team—humankind's team. The world would be our stadium, and we'd always have each other's back. Every day would be a game day in which we gave 110 percent of ourselves to the greater good of humanity.

What a difference in perspective a team mentality would offer if we were each willing to sacrifice our self-interests in pursuit of a common goal! Moreover, a team mentality, predicated on honor, love, and respect, would render racism irrelevant.

Cultural Honor

One of my Middle Eastern Chaldean *sistas* told me about weddings in her culture. All the female family members and close friends of the bride participate in a ceremony days before the wedding. These women dip their hands in henna until the color soaks in. The length of the soak depends on how many days there are until the wedding begins.

This tradition is performed to designate the women as part of the bride's inner circle. This ceremony isn't just for show: the women make a public statement that they are there to support the bride. The women are a source of love, encouragement, and accountability for the bride. Although the henna eventually wears off, their commitment does not.

I think anyone would agree that this is a beautiful cultural expression of love. Imagine the countless other traditions we can celebrate and incorporate to enrich our lives and our culture. Culture is the way we do things. How do you demonstrate your commitment to your friends? How do you remind them of your availability to them and their significance to you?

Crossing Cultures

Since cultural expressions are not perfect, we shouldn't let human culture inhibit God's dreams for our lives. If a culture embraces dishonor, that element must be confronted and removed. For example, Steve, the Mexican guy I shared about earlier in this chapter, served his sentence and one day found himself in a church, listening to a Black preacher.

I could be friends with that guy, Steve thought.

This sentiment was totally against Steve's prison culture, but not against his God-given calling to honor his brother. We ended up becoming friends and partnering in ministry for many years.

Yes, that preacher Steve listened to is me.

Today Steve lives beyond the message of exclusion, one that almost enslaved him into living a life below his full potential. For three decades Steve has helped teenagers from all racial and ethnic groups move past cultural differences and personal pain to become the people God called them to be.

Steve's cultural barriers weren't strong enough to keep us apart. And I'm grateful for the impact he's had on thousands of people, including me.

Next Steps

1. Since culture is "how we do things," identify one cultural practice you have that hinders you from getting to know or honor those who are different from you.

2. Have a conversation with someone from a different culture about something you can both relate to: parenting, sports, career development, or relationship struggles. Ask for their opinion, perspective, or experience on the issue.

3. Identify one cultural practice you've learned from another that has enriched your life.

Prayer

"That which has been is what will be,
That which is done is what will be done,
And there is nothing new under the sun." (Ecclesiastes 1:9)

Dear Lord, open my eyes to see the beauty of your creative expression in other cultures. Reveal to me what you want me to learn from them. I humble myself before You and Your way of doing things. Show me how to engage in conversation that will honor the experiences of others. Teach my heart to learn from and build bridges with those whose experiences are different than mine. We are all trying to do the same things, just in different ways. There is nothing new. Help us learn from each other.

In Your name I pray, Amen.

CHAPTER 18

Red

The color of honor.

Sean was at the Padres baseball game in San Diego when a little kid he'd never met before walked up and started hammering him with questions.

"My name's Timothy. What's your name?"

"How old do you think I am?"

"Guess where I live! Starts with an *S*."

"Do you go to a lot of games?"

Sean got all the answers wrong, and was getting a little irritated when Timothy said, "Are you a Christian?" Sean was now fully engaged.

Sean said, "Why, yes. I am."

"You know we're all one big family, right?"

"Right." As Sean tried to process the conversation, someone distracted him for a moment. But out of the corner of his eye, he saw Timothy lifting his shirt over his head. *What the heck is this child doing?* he wondered.

"Three Thanksgivings ago, I got a new heart! See?"

Sean looked down at the long, brutal scar where they opened up his small chest as Timothy chirped up again. "People tell me that my new heart was a gift. I think it's a gift, too. It was a gift from a girl. She was Black, you know. We're all here together at the game, and it doesn't matter if you have dark skin and I have light skin, right?"

With tears in his eyes, Sean stuttered, "What an amazing gift you've got, Timothy. You're right again, it doesn't matter what color our skin is."

Timothy waved good-bye and said, "It feels like you're part of my family. I don't mean the human family, I mean like my close family. I love you!"

Timothy realized that the only color that mattered to him—the color that gave him life—was red, the color of the new heart in his chest. And it didn't matter to him whether that heart came from someone who looked like him or not. Timothy embodied a Third Option perspective that we should all adopt: God's honoring perspective on all of us as members of the same family—His.

The Greatest Gift Is a New Heart

God created us in His image so we can share His heart. He wants to hear His heart beat in our loving and honoring posture toward each other.

God made us in His image, but we all need a new heart. This is why Jesus Christ endured the pain of crucifixion: to remove all barriers between God and human kind, and to offer us new hearts. But a new heart isn't transferred automatically; it's waiting to be received by you. If you recognize that you need a new heart—the heart of God—receiving it is as simple as A, B, C.

A: Admit that you need help. The Bible says that "all have sinned and fall short of the glory of God" (Romans 3:23). This means that you are not perfect. I don't think that's a real stretch to admit, do you?

B: Believe that Jesus Christ is Lord. The Bible also says that "God so loved the world that He gave His only begotten Son, that whoever believes in Him shall not perish but have everlasting life" (John 3:16). Believing is the key to receiving.

C: Confess what you believe. Romans 10:9–10 says, "If you confess with your mouth, 'Jesus is Lord,' and believe in your heart that God raised him from the dead, you will be saved. For it is with your heart that you believe and are justified, and it is with your mouth that you confess and are saved."

1 John 1:9 says, "If we confess our sins, He is faithful and just to forgive us our sins and to cleanse us from all unrighteousness."

God created you to have a relationship with Him. If you understand that Jesus' death on the cross was to pay for *your* sins and not His own, and if you'd like to personally ask Jesus to forgive you in order to give you His heart, simply pray this prayer:

Dear God, I admit that I'm a sinner and that the penalty of my sin is death. I believe that Jesus Christ is Lord, and He died and rose from the dead for my sin. I confess Jesus as my Savior. Please forgive me. I repent of my sin and surrender my life to you. Fill me with the Spirit of God, and give me a new heart.

I pray this all in Jesus' name, Amen.

If you prayed that prayer with me, please contact me at sdrock.com/knowgod so I can send you a free gift for making this life-changing decision today.

Oh, and welcome to the family.

The Greatest Gift from a New Heart Is Honor

When we honor our Creator by choosing the Third Option, we receive His heart, which equips us to engage with others. And when we fail at engaging in love, we also recognize that every day is a new opportunity to start again.

Give yourself permission to move away from social narratives—the stories you've believed about your life and the attitudes of others—if they include racial bias. There is much more to who you are and who "they" are than any narrative apart from God's can capture.

Ask God to help you choose the Third Option every day, so that you see people from His perspective. By doing so, you will come to recognize each person as valuable, created in God's image, and desiring of the same life, liberty, and happiness as you.

Decide and take proactive measures to learn about other people and yourself. Step out in faith, awkward as it may feel, and ask honest questions. You're guaranteed to make mistakes, so give yourself permission to make them, and grant others the same grace you extend yourself whenever they make theirs.

Acknowledge your feelings—which will range from fear to excitement—as you take proactive steps to honor people. Your actions, your feelings, and your honesty will make a lasting impression on them.

God has created you to celebrate His diversity as expressed in the cultures of people throughout the world. Soak it all up and savor the goodness of His love by sharing it with everyone you meet.

Next Steps

1. Pray for courage to live out what you have learned.
2. Tell someone what you have learned from reading this book.

3. Share something about this book with someone in person or on social media.

Prayer

"Then I will give them one heart, and I will put a new spirit within them, and take the stony heart out of their flesh, and give them a heart of flesh, that they may walk in My statutes and keep My judgments and do them; and they shall be My people, and I will be their God." (Ezekiel 11:19–20)

Dear God, please grant me a new heart, one that embraces and puts into practice what I have learned from this book. Use me to bring about change in my world. Unity starts with me. Help me to choose the Third Option of honor, and teach me to love and value all people, no matter what they look like or where they come from. In Jesus' name, Amen.

1. http://www.pewresearch.org/fact-tank/2017/08/29/views-of
   -racism-as-a-major-problem-increase-sharply-especially-among
   -democrats.
2. Mayor, Susan. "Genome Sequence of One Individual is Published
   for First Time." US National Library of Medicine, September 15,
   2007.
3. https://study.com/academy/lesson/the-one-drop-rule-in
   -american-history.html.
4. https://www.usatoday.com/story/news/nation/2013/11/21
   /White-supremacist-dna-test-neo-nazi-north-dakota-town
   /3661791.
5. https://www.adl.org/racism.
6. Phyllis Jones, Camara. "Levels of Racism: A Theoretic Frame-
   work and a Gardener's Tale." *American Journal of Public Health*,
   August 2000.
7. https://www.theatlantic.com/national/archive/2011/11/racist
   -anti-immigrant-cartoons-from-the-turn-of-the-20th-century
   /383248.
8. http://www.history.com/news/when-america-despised-the
   -irish-the-19th-centurys-refugee-crisis.
9. https://www.nbcnews.com/news/latino/history-racism-against
   -mexican-americans-clouds-texas-immigration-law-n766956.

10. http://www.slate.com/blogs/the_vault/2014/05/30/where_
    to_find_historical_redlining_maps_of_your_city.html

11. https://en.wikipedia.org/wiki/Ingroups_and_outgroups.

12. https://en.wikipedia.org/wiki/Shaker_Heights_High_School.

13. http://www.aei.org/publication/closing-the-racial-gap-in
    -education/ and http://www.nytimes.com/2005/12/14/educa
    tion/how-one-suburbs-black-students-gain.html?_r=0.

14. http://crossroadsantiracism.org/antiracism-analysis/blindspot
    -hidden-biases-of-good-people-a-review/ and https://www.amazon
    .com/Blindspot-Hidden-Biases-Good-People/dp/0345528433.

15. Chadiha, Kizza. "State of Science on Unconscious Bias." UCSF
    Office of Diversity and Outreach. https://diversity.ucsf.edu
    /resources/state-science-unconscious-bias (Accessed March 4,
    2017).

16. McCormick, Horace. *The Real Effects of Unconscious Bias
    in the Workplace.* https://www.kenan-flagler.unc.edu/~/media
    /Files/documents/executive-development/unc-White-paper
    -the-real-effects-of-unconscious-bias-in-the-workplace-Final
    (Accessed March 4, 2017).

17. Dixon, T. L. & Linz, D. G. "Overrepresentation and Under-
    representation of African Americans and Latinos as Lawbreakers on
    Television News." *Journal of Communication*, 50(2), 131–54; Gilliam,
    F. D. & Iyengar, S. (2000).

18. Dixon, T. L. & Linz, D. G. "Race and the Misrepresentation
    of Victimization on Local Television News," *Communication
    Research* 27(5), 547–73, (2000).

19. Romer, D., Jamieson, K. H., & de Coteau, N. J. "The Treatment
    of Persons of Color in Local Television News: Ethnic Blame
    Discourse or Realistic Group Conflict?" *Communication Research*,
    25(3), 268–305, (1998).

20. http://www.sentencingproject.org/wp-content/uploads/2015/11/Race-and-Punishment.pdf, p. 22.

21. Dana Mastro and Maria Kopacz, "Media Representations of Race, Prototypicality, and Policy Reasoning: An Application of Self-Categorization Theory," *Journal of Broadcasting and Electronic Media*, June 2006, p. 306.

22. http://www.cbsnews.com/news/on-the-road-innocent-michigan-man-ends-up-working-alongside-crooked-cop-that-locked-him.

23. William H. Willimon, *Fear of the Other: No Fear in Love* (Nashville: Abingdon Press, 2016), 23.

24. Ibid.

25. https://www.washingtonpost.com/news/wonk/wp/2014/08/25/three-quarters-of-Whites-dont-have-any-non-White-friends/?utm_term=.47318c4f881e.

26. http://www.jonesandassociatesconsulting.com.

27. http://tools.acc.org/ascvd-risk-estimator.

28. https://www.washingtonpost.com/news/wonk/wp/2015/05/28/evidence-that-banks-still-deny-black-borrowers-just-as-they-did-50-years-ago/?utm_term=.3adc60f4f91c.

29. http://www.efc.gwu.edu/library/disparities-between-urban-and-suburban-schools.

30. http://www.slate.com/articles/news_and_politics/crime/2015/08/racial_disparities_in_the_criminal_justice_system_eight_charts_illustrating.html.

31. https://sociology.fas.harvard.edu/people/devah-pager and https://scholar.harvard.edu/pager/publications1.

32. https://today.duke.edu/2012/04/jurystudy.

33. Human Rights Watch, "The New Jim Crow," *Punishment and Prejudice: Racial Disparities on the War on Drugs*, vol. 12 2 (May 2000):99.

34. http://www.star-telegram.com/sports/article3849895.html.

35. http://www.cnn.com/2017/05/19/health/myron-rolle-nfl -medical-school-profile/index.html.

36. Hiebert, Paul G. *Transforming Worldviews: An Anthropological Understanding of How People Change.* Grand Rapids, MI: Baker Academic, 2008.

I would like to acknowledge and give thanks to the following friends and family members, who inspired and encouraged me along the way:

- ❖ My Lord and Savior, Jesus Christ, for loving me unconditionally

- ❖ My parents and grandparents, who modeled walking in love and pain

- ❖ My wife, Debbie, who had to listen to these stories and insights every day for the past two years and still loves me in spite of it

- ❖ My family, for always supporting and encouraging me through every season of my life

- ❖ The Rock Church staff, for praying for and struggling through this process with me

- ❖ The Rock Church congregation for the courage to live these truths out every day since our birth as a church family in 2000

- ❖ My board, for their support and encouragement

- ❖ The Fedd Agency, for their expertise in guiding me through this process

- ❖ Dr. Green and Dr. Hood, for your invaluable expertise and insight, which transformed the contents of this book

- ❖ My writers and researchers, for helping me do what I could not do

- Denise, for your amazing insight and expertise

- Everyone who has poured into my life over the years, encouraging me to believe in myself and trust in God

- Everyone who hurt and criticized me. Your words, actions, and discrimination were meant for evil, but God turned them into something great

- Everyone who reads this book, for caring about the plight of their neighbors, and seeking to honor and love them better— may God bless you on your journey